١٠٠ حديث عن الآداب الإسلامية

100 AHADITH ABOUT ISLAMIC MANNERS

Compiled by

Research Division, Darussalam

دار السلام
DARUSSALAM

DARUSSALAM
GLOBAL LEADER IN ISLAMIC BOOKS
Riyadh • Jeddah • Al-Khobar • Sharjah
Lahore • London • Houston • Newyork

بسم الله الرحمن الرحيم

In the Name of Allâh
The Most Beneficent, the Most Merciful

١٠٠ حديث عن الآداب الإسلامية

100 AHADITH

ABOUT ISLAMIC MANNERS

Second Edition: October 2003

King Fahd National Library Cataloging-in-Publication Data
Maktaba Dar-us-Salam
100 Ahadith about islamic manners-Riyadh.
80p., 14x21 cm.
ISBN 9960-717-72-0
I-Islam -General Principles II-Title
243 dc. 4591/21
Legal Deposit no. 4591/21
ISBN 9960-717-72-0

Headoffice: P.O. Box: 22743, Riyadh 11416 K.S.A. Tel: 00966-01-4033962/4043432 Fax: 4021659
E-mail: darussalam@awalnet.net.sa Website: http// www.dar-us-salam.com

K.S.A. Darussalam Showrooms:
Riyadh
Olaya branch: Tel 00966-1-4614483 Fax: 4644945
Malaz branch: Tel 4735220 Fax: 4735221
- Jeddah
  Tel: 00966-2-6879254 Fax: 6336270
- Al-Khobar
  Tel: 00966-3-8692900 Fax: 00966-3-8691551

U.A.E
- Darussalam, Sharjah U.A.E
  Tel: 00971-6-5632623 Fax: 5632624

PAKISTAN
- Darussalam, 36 B Lower Mall, Lahore
  Tel: 0092-42-724 0024 Fax: 7354072
- Rahman Market, Ghazni Street
  Urdu Bazar Lahore
  Tel: 0092-42-7120054 Fax: 7320703

U.S.A
- Darussalam, Houston
  P.O Box: 79194 Tx 772779
  Tel: 001-713-722 0419 Fax: 001-713-722 0431
  E-mail: sales@dar-us-salam.com
- Darussalam, New York
  572 Atlantic Ave, Brooklyn
  New York-11217, Tel: 001-718-625 5925

U.K
- Darussalam International Publications Ltd.
  226 High Street, Walthamstow,
  London E17 7JH, Tel: 0044-208 520 2666
  Mobile: 0044-794 730 6706 Fax: 0044-208 521 7645
- Darussalam International Publications Limited
  Regent Park Mosque, 146 Park Road,
  London NW8 7RG Tel: 0044-207 724 3363
- Darussalam
  398-400 Coventry Road, Small Heath
  Birmingham, B10 0UF
  Tel: 0121 77204792 Fax: 0121 772 4345
  E-mail: info@darussalamuk.com
  Web: www.darussalamuk.com

FRANCE
- Editions & Librairie Essalam
  135, Bd de Ménilmontant- 75011 Paris
  Tél: 0033-01- 43 38 19 56/ 44 83
  Fax: 0033-01- 43 57 44 31
  E-mail: essalam@essalam.com

AUSTRALIA
- ICIS: Ground Floor 165-171, Haldon St.
  Lakemba NSW 2195, Australia
  Tel: 00612 9758 4040 Fax: 9758 4030

MALAYSIA
- E&D Books SDN. BHD.-321 B 3rd Floor,
  Suria Klcc
  Kuala Lumpur City Center 50088
  Tel: 00603-21663433 Fax: 459 72032

SINGAPORE
- Muslim Converts Association of Singapore
  32 Onan Road The Galaxy Singapore- 424484
  Tel: 0065-440 6924, 348 8344 Fax: 440 6724

SRI LANKA
- Darul Kitab 6, Nimal Road, Colombo-4
  Tel: 0094-1-589 038 Fax: 0094-74 722433

KUWAIT
- Islam Presentation Committee
  Enlightment Book Shop
  P.O. Box: 1613, Safat 13017 Kuwait
  Tel: 00965-244 7526, Fax: 240 0057

INDIA
- Islamic Dimensions
  56/58 Tandel Street (North)
  Dongri, Mumbai 4000 009, India
  Tel: 0091-22-3736875, Fax: 3730689
  E-mail: sales@IRF.net

SOUTH AFRICA
- Islamic Da'wah Movement (IDM)
  48009 Qualbert 4078 Durban, South Africa
  Tel: 0027-31-304-6883
  Fax: 0027-31-305-1292
  E-mail: idm@ion.co.za

Contents

The Messenger of Allâh ﷺ Says:

"Abdullâh bin Mas'ud رضي الله عنه narrated that the Prophet ﷺ said, 'May Allâh brighten the face of that person who heard anything from us then carried it accordingly to others. There are many persons who remember it better than those who conveyed it to them.' " (*At-Tirmidhi*)

Publishers Note

All the praises are due to Allâh, the Lord of the worlds, and may Allâh send prayers of blessings upon Prophet Muhammad, the chosen, the trustworthy, and upon his family and all of his companions.

'100 Ahâdîth about Islâmic Manners' is a part of our new package for Muslims. There are two main sources of the *Sharî'ah* - the Qur'ân and the *Hadîth.* The traditions of the Prophet ﷺ inform us about the practical aspects of Divine commandments for human life and provide explanations and demonstrations of the basic principles. Due to the importance of this second source, we are presenting this collection.

We try to present our publications based on authentic research material in accordance with the Qur'ân and Sunnah, along with simplicity and freedom from every type of vague conception, weak authority, and false ideas. You will find the same spirit and tradition of good research, professional editing and excellent printing standard in this work.

This collection of *Ahâdîth* relates to the important aspects of daily life so that the readers may benefit from it for their success in this life as well as in hereafter.

May Allâh accept our sincere efforts regarding the propagation of His religion throughout the world, and bestow on us His blessings to fulfil our resolution in this regard. *Amîn!*

Abdul Malik Mujahid
General Manager

The Importance of Ahâdîth

There are two main sources of the religion of Islâm: the Qur'ân and the Traditions of the Prophet Muhammad ﷺ *(Ahâdîth* and *Sunnah*). The Qur'ân was revealed to the Messenger of Allâh ﷺ during the period of 611CE to 632CE for all of mankind, and he ﷺ conveyed the Word of Allâh as it is to his Ummah (nation or followers). In this Divine Message there is a complete way of life. It means that the Allâh has directly revealed the correct way of life for all of mankind. This (the Qur'ân) is the main source of success in this world and the hereafter.

The other source of guidance is called *Hadîth* or *Sunnah* of the Prophet ﷺ. It means the sayings, deeds and approvals accurately narrated from the Prophet ﷺ. There is a ruling from Allâh concerning the traditions of His Messenger ﷺ:

> "Nor does he speak from (his own) desire. It is only a Revelation revealed." (53:3,4)

And He said:

> "Oh you who believe! Obey Allâh, and obey the Messenger (Muhammad ﷺ)...." (47:33)

He also said:

> "He who obeys the Messenger (Muhammad ﷺ), has indeed obeyed Allâh..." (4:80)

And in the same sense Allâh said about His Messenger ﷺ:

> "Indeed in the Messenger of Allâh (Muhammad ﷺ) you have a good example to follow ..." (33:21)

And the Messenger of Allâh ﷺ said:

> "Every new thing in Islâm is *Bid'ah* (any innovated practice in religion) and every *Bid'ah* is misguidance."

He (ﷺ) also said: "Whoever obeys me will enter Paradise."

According to these traditions, every Muslim should read the *Ahâdîth* and follow the good example of the Messenger of Allâh ﷺ. If we made the aim to follow his guidance in our daily routine work, we can live a good and successful life in this world and the hereafter.

There is a good example in the Prophet's *Sunnah*. He practiced it in his lifetime and his Companions also practiced it. Likewise, it is possible to follow it in every age. So it is necessary for all the Muslims to act upon these traditions.

We should learn these *Ahâdîth* and the *Sunnah* to implement in our daily and nightly routine.

Prophet Muhammad ﷺ usually delivered a Khutbah about the different manners and the lifestyle. These sayings of the Prophet ﷺ were collected by his Companions. Many of them learned them by heart and some of them wrote them down. However, the written *Ahâdîth* were not in great number. After the Prophet Muhammad ﷺ, the Companions collected the *Ahâdîth* and wrote them as correctly as possible. In the second and third generation of the Muslims, this work was done as much as possible but most of them were learned by heart. After them there were Imâms (great scholars) who collected the *Ahâdîth* and wrote them with classifications based on the level of authenticity of the *Ahâdîth.* They developed the Science of *Hadîth,* and by analysing the various methods, sources and personalities who were involved in the collections of the *Ahâdîth,* they developed ways to judge the correctness and the authenticity of the *Ahâdîth.* The purpose of this was to eliminate any false information or narration and sift these narrations from the correct ones. According to the strength of the authenticity, the *Ahâdîth* were classified differently. Some of the most important kinds of *Ahâdîth* are classified as follows:

Dha'îf (weak): An inaccurate narration which does not meet the qualifications of being either *Sahîh* (sound) or *Hasan* (fair), and hence cannot be used as a basis of an Islâmic opinion.

Gharîb (unfamiliar or rare): A Hadîth or version reported by one reliable or unreliable narrator which was not reported by others. The Hadîth may be *Gharîb* in the text of its wording, in some of its wording (such as additional words), or in its chain of narrators. A *Gharîb Hadîth* can be *Sahîh* (sound) or *Dha'îf* (weak).

Hasan (good or fair): A *Musnad Hadîth* narrated by a reliable chain, but not reaching the grade of *Sahîh* (sound) *Hadîth.*

Majhûl (unknown): If there is an unknown person in the chain of narrators of a Hadîth.

Maqtû' (disconnected): (i) A *Hadîth* ending at a *Tâbi'i* by both action and words. (ii) A *Hadîth* with an incomplete chain of narrators. (iii) A *Hadîth* in which a *Sahâbi* describes about something by saying, 'we used to do...'

Marfû' (traceable): A *Hadîth* referred to the Prophet ﷺ, be it a saying or an action, whether *Muttasil* (connected) or *Munqati'* (disconnected).

Mawqûf (untraceable): A *Hadîth* from a *Sahâbi* (Comapanion of the Prophet ﷺ). It is a description, report or information given by a *Sahâbi* that he does not attribute to the Prophet ﷺ. A *Mawqûf* narration is also called an *Athar.*

Munqati' (disconnected): A *Hadîth* with an incomplete chain of narrators or containing in its chain an unknown reporter.

Mursal (disreferred): A *Hadîth* with the chain of narrators ending at a *Tâbi'i* who quotes directly from the Prophet ﷺ without referring to the Companion from whom he heard it.

Muttasil (connected) or *Mawsul*: A *Hadîth* with a complete chain of narrators until it reaches its source. It can either be *Marfû'* (traceable) referring to the Prophet ﷺ, or *Mawquf* (untraceable) ending at a *Sahâbi.*

Sahîh (sound): A *Musnad Hadîth* with an unbroken chain of narrators; one narrated from all reliable reporters with good memory back to tne source without being *Shâth* (strange and defective) or *Mu'allal* (faulty).

With the Name of Allâh, the Most Gracious, the Most Merciful

بسمِ الله الرَّحْمٰن الرَّحِيم

Preordainment of Allāh

1. Ibn Abbâs رضي الله عنهما said: One day, I was riding behind the Prophet ﷺ when he said, "O boy! I will teach you some words. Be mindful of Allâh (Commandments of Allâh), He will preserve you. Be mindful of Allâh, He will be ever with you. If you beg, beg of Him Alone; and if you need assistance, supplicate to Allâh Alone for help. And know that if all the people gather to benefit you, they will not be able to benefit you except that which Allâh had preordained (for you); and if all of them gather to do harm to you, they will not be able to afflict you with anything other than that which Allâh had pre-destined against you. The pens have been lifted and the ink of the pages has dried up." [*At-Tirmidhî*]

Another narration states: The Messenger of Allâh ﷺ said, "Safeguard (the Commandments of) Allâh, you will find Him before you. Remember Him in prosperity and He will remember you in adversity. Know that whatever you miss, was not destined to befall you; and what befalls you, was never going to miss you. Know that the Help (of Allâh) is obtained with patience, happiness

١ - عَن ابْنِ عَبَّاسٍ، رَضِيَ الله عَنْهُمَا، قال: كُنْتُ خلفَ النَّبيِّ، ﷺ، يَوْمًا فَقَالَ: «يَا غُلامُ! إِنِّي أُعَلِّمُكَ كَلِمَاتٍ: احْفَظِ الله يَحْفَظْكَ، احْفَظِ الله تَجِدْهُ تُجَاهَكَ، إِذَا سَأَلْتَ فَاسْأَلِ الله، وَإِذَا اسْتَعَنْتَ فَاسْتَعِنْ بالله، وَاعْلَمْ: أَنَّ الأُمَّةَ لَوِ اجْتَمَعَتْ عَلَى أَنْ يَنْفَعُوكَ بِشَيْءٍ، لَمْ يَنْفَعُوكَ إِلَّا بِشَيْءٍ قَدْ كَتَبَهُ الله لَكَ، وَإِنِ اجْتَمَعُوا عَلَى أَنْ يَضُرُّوكَ بِشَيْءٍ؛ لَمْ يَضُرُّوكَ إِلَّا بِشَيْءٍ قَدْ كَتَبَهُ الله عَلَيْكَ؛ رُفِعَتِ الأَقْلَامُ، وَجَفَّتِ الصُّحُفُ» رواهُ التِّرمذيُّ وَقَالَ: حَديثٌ حَسنٌ صحيحٌ.

وَفي روايةِ غَيْرِ التِّرمذيِّ: «احْفَظِ الله تَجِدْهُ أَمَامَكَ، تَعَرَّفْ إِلَى الله فِي الرَّخَاءِ يَعْرِفْكَ فِي الشِّدَّةِ، وَاعْلَمْ أَنَّ مَا أَخْطَأَكَ لَمْ يَكُنْ لِيُصِيبَكَ وَمَا أَصَابَكَ لَمْ يَكُنْ لِيُخْطِئَكَ، وَاعْلَمْ أَنَّ النَّصْرَ مَعَ الصَّبْرِ، وَأَنَّ الْفَرَجَ مَعَ

comes after distress, and hardship is followed by ease."

الْكَرْبِ، وَأَنَّ مَعَ الْعُسْرِ يُسْرًا».

Commentary:

1. No one has the power to change the Decision of Allâh.
2. Whatever trouble one suffers in this world, it does not last for ever. Every trouble is followed by prosperity, pleasure and happiness.
3. One should never ask other than Allâh's help in supernatural things because it amounts to ascribing partnership with Allâh. If a person is mindful of the Rights of Allâh, then Allâh in return takes care of his needs and helps him.

The Right of Allāh upon His Slaves

2. Narrated Mu'ādh bin Jabal رَضِيَ اللهُ عَنْهُما: The Prophet ﷺ said, "O Mu'ādh! Do you know what Allāh's Right upon His slaves is?" I said, "Allāh and His Messenger know better." The Prophet ﷺ said, "That they worship Him (Allāh) Alone and do not associate any partner in worship with Him (Allāh). Do you know what their right upon Him is?" I replied, "Allāh and His Messenger know better." The Prophet ﷺ said, "That He will not punish them (if they did so)." [*Al-Bukhāri*]

٢ - عَنْ مُعاذِ بنِ جَبَلٍ قالَ: قالَ النَّبِيُّ ﷺ: «يا مُعاذُ، أتَدْرِي ما حَقُّ اللهِ عَلى العِبادِ؟» قالَ: اللهُ وَرَسُولُهُ أعْلَمُ، قالَ: «أنْ يَعْبُدُوهُ وَلا يُشْرِكوا بِهِ شَيْئاً. أتَدْري ما حَقُّهُمْ عَلَيهِ؟» قالَ: اللهُ ورَسُولُهُ أعْلَمُ. قالَ: «أنْ لا يُعَذِّبَهُمْ».

The Rights of a Muslim

3. Abû Hurairah رضي الله عنه reported: The Messenger of Allâh ﷺ said, "Every Muslim has five rights over another Muslim (i.e., he has to perform five duties regarding another Muslim): to return the greetings, to visit the sick, to accompany funeral

٣ - عَنْ أَبِي هُرَيْرَةَ، رَضِيَ اللهُ عَنْهُ، أَنَّ رَسُولَ اللهِ، ﷺ، قالَ: «حَقُّ الْمُسْلِمِ عَلَى الْمُسْلِمِ خَمْسٌ: رَدُّ السَّلامِ، وَعِيادَةُ المَرِيضِ، وَاتِّباعُ الجَنَائِزِ، وإجابَةُ الدَّعْوَةِ، وتَشْمِيتُ

processions, to accept an invitation, and to respond to the sneezer [i.e., to say: '*Yarhamuk-Allâh* (may Allâh bestow His Mercy on you)' when the sneezer praises Allâh]." [*Al-Bukhârî* and *Muslim*]

الْعَاطِسِ» متفقٌ عليه .

Commentary: The bond of fraternity among the Muslims has been further strengthened by the list in this *Hadīth* about the rights of Muslims on one another.

Obedience of the Prophet Muhammad ﷺ

4. Narrated Ibn 'Umar رضي الله عنهما: Whenever we took an oath of allegiance to the Messenger of Allâh ﷺ to hear and obey, he (ﷺ) would say to us, "As much as you are able."

[*Al-Bukhârî* and *Muslim*]

٤- عَن ابنِ عُمَرَ رَضِيَ الله عَنْهُمَا قال: كُنَّا إِذَا بَايَعْنَا رَسُولَ الله ﷺ عَلَى السَّمْعِ وَالطَّاعَةِ يَقُولُ لَنَا: «فِيمَا اسْتَطَعْتُمْ» متفقٌ عَلَيه .

Commentary: Obedience to a Muslim ruler calls for two conditions: First, his command must not transgress the sacred law of the religion; second, it should not go beyong people's limitations. In case, he fails to meet these two prerequisites, his obedience will also become non-obligatory. This *Hadîth* conveys a warning to rulers that they must not put people to hardships unbearable to them.

5. Abû Hurairah رضي الله عنه reported: The Messenger of Allâh ﷺ said, "Everyone of my *Ummah* will enter *Jannah* except those who refuse." He was asked: "Who will refuse?" He ﷺ said, "Whoever obeys me shall enter *Jannah*, and whosoever disobeys me refuses to (enter *Jannah*)."

[*Al-Bukhârî*]

٥ - عَنْ أَبِي هُرَيْرَةَ رَضِيَ الله عَنْهُ أَنَّ رَسُولَ الله ﷺ قَالَ: «كُلُّ أُمَّتِي يَدْخُلُونَ الْجَنَّةَ إِلَّا مَنْ أَبَى». قِيلَ: وَمَنْ يَأْبَى يَا رَسُولَ الله؟ قَالَ: «مَنْ أَطَاعَنِي دَخَلَ الجنَّةَ، وَمَنْ عَصَانِي فَقَدْ أَبَى» رواه الْبُخَارِي .

Commentary: The word *Ummah* here means the community which accepted the invitation of the Prophet ﷺ, that is to say, the people who on his call embraced Islâm. All of this community who follow him faithfully will go to *Jannah*.

Da'wah Priorities

6. Narrated Ibn 'Abbās رَضِيَ اللهُ عَنْهُما: When the Prophet ﷺ sent Mu'ādh to Yemen, he said to him, "You are going to a nation from the people of the Scripture, so let the first thing to which you invite them be to testify to the *Tauhīd* of Allāh [i.e., *Lā ilāha illallāh* (none has the right to be worshipped but Allāh)]. If they accept that, tell them that Allāh has enjoined on them five compulsory congregational *Ṣalāt* (prayers) to be offered in one day and one night (24 hours). And if they offer their *Salāt* (prayer), tell them that Allāh has enjoined on them *Zakāt* of their properties; and it is to be taken from the rich among them and given to the poor among them. And if they agree to that, then take from them *Zakāt*, but avoid the best property of the people." [*Al-Bukhāri*]

٦ - عَن ابنَ عَبَّاسٍ يَقُولُ: لَمَّا بَعَثَ النَّبِيُّ ﷺ مُعاذاً إلى نَحْوِ أَهْلِ اليَمَنِ قالَ لهُ: «إنَّكَ تَقْدَمُ عَلى قَوْمٍ مِنْ أَهْلِ الكِتابِ، فَلْيَكُنْ أَوَّلَ ما تَدْعوهُمْ إلَى أنْ يُوَحِّدُوا اللهَ تَعالَى. فَإذا عَرَفوا ذلكَ فَأَخْبِرْهُمْ أنَّ اللهَ فَرَضَ عَلَيْهِمْ خَمْسَ صَلَواتٍ في يَوْمِهِمْ وَلَيْلَتِهِمْ فَإذا صَلَّوا فَأخبرهُمْ أنَّ اللهَ افْتَرَضَ عَلَيهِمْ زَكاةً في أمْوالِهِمْ تُؤْخَذُ مِنْ غَنِيِّهِمْ فَتُرَدُّ عَلى فَقِيرِهِمْ. فَإذَا أَقَرُّوا بذلِكَ فَخُذْ مِنهُمْ وتَوَقَّ كَرائِمَ أمْوالِ النَّاسِ».

Significance of Intention

7. 'Umar bin Al-Khattâb رضي الله عنه reported: The Messenger of Allâh ﷺ said, "Deeds are considered by intentions, and a person will be rewarded according to his intention. So whoever emigrated for Allāh and His Messenger, his emigration would be for Allāh and His Messenger; and whoever

٧ - وَعَنْ أَمِيرِ الْمُؤْمِنِينَ أَبِي حَفْصٍ عُمَرَ بْنِ الْخَطَّابِ رَضِي الله عنه، قَالَ: سَمِعْتُ رَسُولَ اللهِ ﷺ يَقُولُ: «إِنَّمَا الأَعْمَالُ بالنِّيَّاتِ، وَإِنَّمَا لِكُلِّ امْرِىءٍ مَا نَوَى فَمَنْ كَانَتْ هِجْرَتُهُ إِلَى اللهِ وَرَسُولِهِ فَهِجْرَتُهُ إِلَى اللهِ وَرَسُولِهِ،

emigrated for worldly benefits or for a woman to marry, his emigration would be for what he emigrated for." [*Al-Bukhârî* and *Muslim*]

وَمَنْ كَانَتْ هِجْرَتُهُ لِدُنْيَا يُصِيبُهَا، أَوِ امْرَأَةٍ يَنْكِحُهَا فَهِجْرَتُهُ إِلَى مَا هَاجَرَ إِلَيْهِ» مُتَّفَقٌ عَلَى صِحَتِهِ.

Commentary: According to some *Ahadîth*, the reason for this *Hadîth* is that a person sent a proposal of marriage to a woman named Umm Qais, which she turned down saying that he would have to emigrate to Al-Madinah to marry her. Accordingly, he did it for this specific purpose, and the two were married there. On account of this event, the man came to be known among the Companions as *Muhâjir Umm Qais*.

On the basis of this *Hadîth*, *'Ulamâ'* are of the unanimous opinion that the real basis of one's actions is *Niyyah* (intention) and everyone will be requited according to his *Niyyah*. It is true that *Niyyah* is founded in one's heart, that is to say, one has first to make up one's mind for what he intends to do and he should not express it verbally. In fact, the latter is a *Bid'ah* (innovation in religion) because no proof of it is found in the *Sharî'ah*.

The point which becomes evident from this *Hadîth* is that *Ikhlâs* (sincerity) is a must for every action. In other words, in every righteous deed, one should seek only the Pleasure of Allâh; otherwise, it will not be accepted by Allâh.

The Effects of Strong Faith

8. Suhaib رضي الله عنه reported that the Messenger of Allâh ﷺ said, "There lived a king before you and he had a court magician. As he (the magician) grew old, he said to the king: 'I have grown old, so send me a young boy so that I may teach him magic.' The king sent him a young boy to serve the purpose. And on his way (to the magician) the young boy met a monk to whom he listened to and he liked his speech. It became his habit that on his way to the magician, he would meet

٨ - وَعَنْ صُهَيْبٍ رضي الله عَنْهُ أَنَّ رسول الله ﷺ قال: «كَانَ مَلِكٌ فِيمَنْ كَانَ قَبْلَكُمْ، وَكَانَ لَهُ سَاحِرٌ، فَلَمَّا كَبِرَ قَالَ لِلْمَلِكِ: إِنِّي قَدْ كَبِرْتُ فَابْعَثْ إِلَيَّ غُلامًا أُعَلِّمْهُ السِّحْرَ؛ فَبَعَثَ إِلَيْهِ غُلامًا يُعَلِّمُهُ، وَكَانَ فِي طَرِيقِهِ إِذَا سَلَكَ رَاهِبٌ، فَقَعَدَ إِلَيْهِ وَسَمِعَ كَلامَهُ فَأَعْجَبَهُ، وَكَانَ إِذَا أَتَى السَّاحِرَ مَرَّ بِالرَّاهِبِ وَقَعَدَ إِلَيْهِ، فَإِذَا

the monk and sit with him and would come to the magician (late). The magician used to beat him because of this delay. He complained about this to the monk who said to him: 'When you feel afraid of the magician, say: My family detained me. And when you fear your family, say: The magician detained me.' So while he was in this state it so happened that a huge beast came and it blocked the way of the people. The young boy said: 'I will know today whether the magician or the monk is better.' He picked up a stone and said: 'O Allâh, if the way of the monk is dearer to You than the way of the magician, kill this animal so that the people may pass.' He threw that stone at it and killed it and the people were able to pass. He then came to the monk and told him the story. The monk said: 'Son, today you are superior to me. You have come to a stage where I feel that you would be soon put to a trial, and in case you are put to a trial, do not reveal me.' That young boy began to heal those born blind and the lepers and he, in fact, began to cure people from all kinds of illness. When a courtier of the king who had gone blind heard about him, he came to him with numerous gifts and said, 'If you cure me, all these things will be yours.' He said, 'I myself do not cure anyone. It is Allâh the Exalted Alone Who cures; and if you

أَتَى السَّاحِرَ ضَرَبَهُ، فَشَكَا ذٰلِكَ إِلَى الرَّاهِبِ فَقَالَ: إِذَا خَشِيتَ السَّاحِرَ فَقُلْ: حَبَسَنِي أَهْلِي، وإِذَا خَشِيتَ أَهْلَكَ فَقُلْ: حَبَسَنِي السَّاحِرُ. فَبَيْنَمَا هُوَ عَلَى ذٰلِكَ إِذْ أَتَى عَلَى دَابَّةٍ عَظِيمَةٍ قَدْ حَبَسَتِ النَّاسَ فَقَالَ: الْيَوْمَ أَعْلَمُ آلسَّاحِرُ أَفْضَلُ أَمِ الرَّاهِبُ أَفْضَلُ؟ فَأَخَذَ حَجَرًا فَقَالَ: اللَّهُمَّ إِنْ كَانَ أَمْرُ الرَّاهِبِ أَحَبَّ إِلَيْكَ مِنْ أَمْرِ السَّاحِرِ فَاقْتُلْ هٰذِهِ الدَّابَّةَ حَتَّى يَمْضِيَ النَّاسُ، فَرَمَاهَا فَقَتَلَهَا وَمَضَى النَّاسُ، فَأَتَى الرَّاهِبَ فَأَخْبَرَهُ. فَقَالَ لَهُ الرَّاهِبُ: أَيْ بُنَيَّ أَنْتَ الْيَوْمَ أَفْضَلُ مِنِّي، قَدْ بَلَغَ مِنْ أَمْرِكَ مَا أَرَى، وَإِنَّكَ سَتُبْتَلَى، فَإِنِ ابْتُلِيتَ فَلا تَدُلَّ عَلَيَّ؛ وَكَانَ الْغُلامُ يُبْرِىءُ الأَكْمَهَ وَالأَبْرَصَ، وَيُدَاوِي النَّاسَ مِنْ سَائِرِ الأَدْوَاءِ. فَسَمِعَ جَلِيسٌ لِلْمَلِكِ كَانَ قَدْ عَمِيَ، فَأَتَاهُ بِهَدَايَا كَثِيرَةٍ فَقَالَ: مَا هَا هُنَا لَكَ أَجْمَعُ إِنْ أَنْتَ شَفَيْتَنِي، فَقَالَ: إِنِّي لا أَشْفِي أَحَدًا، إِنَّمَا يَشْفِي اللهُ تَعَالَى، فَإِنْ آمَنْتَ بِاللهِ تَعَالَى دَعَوْتُ اللهَ فَشَفَاكَ، فَآمَنَ بِاللهِ تَعَالَى فَشَفَاهُ

affirm faith in Allâh, I shall also supplicate to Allâh to cure you.' This courtier affirmed his faith in Allâh and Allâh cured him. He came to the king and sat by his side as he used to sit before. The king said to him, 'Who restored your eyesight?' He said, 'My Lord.' Thereupon he said, 'Do you have another lord besides me?' He said, 'My Lord and your Lord is Allâh.' So the king seized him and kept torturing him until he revealed the young boy. The young boy was thus brought and the king said to him, 'O boy, has your magic become so proficient that you cure the blind and the lepers and you do such and such?' Thereupon he said, 'I do not cure anyone; it is Allâh Alone Who cures,' and the king took hold of him and began to torture him until he revealed the monk. The monk was brought and it was said to him: 'You should turn back from your religion.' But he refused. The king sent for a saw, placed it in the middle of his head and cut him into two parts until he fell down split in half. Then the courtier of the king was brought forward and it was said to him: 'Turn back from your religion.' He too refused, and the saw was placed in the middle of his head and he was sawn into two parts until he fell down split in half. Then the boy was sent for and it was said to him: 'Turn back from your religion.' He

الله تَعَالَى، فَأَتَى الْمَلِكَ فَجَلَسَ إِلَيْهِ كَمَا كَانَ يَجْلِسُ فَقَالَ لَهُ الْمَلِكُ: مَنْ رَدَّ عَلَيْكَ بَصَرَكَ؟ قَالَ: رَبِّي، قَالَ: أَوَ لَكَ رَبٌّ غَيْرِي؟! قَالَ: رَبِّي وَرَبُّكَ اللهُ، فَأَخَذَهُ فَلَمْ يَزَلْ يُعَذِّبُهُ حَتَّى دَلَّ عَلَى الْغُلَامِ، فَجِيءَ بِالْغُلَامِ فَقَالَ لَهُ الْمَلِكُ: أَيْ بُنَيَّ قَدْ بَلَغَ مِنْ سِحْرِكَ مَا تُبْرِىءُ الْأَكْمَهَ وَالْأَبْرَصَ وَتَفْعَلُ وَتَفْعَلُ؟! فَقَالَ: إِنِّي لَا أَشْفِي أَحَدًا، إِنَّمَا يَشْفِي اللهُ تَعَالَى، فَأَخَذَهُ فَلَمْ يَزَلْ يُعَذِّبُهُ حَتَّى دَلَّ عَلَى الرَّاهِبِ؛ فَجِيءَ بِالرَّاهِبِ فَقِيلَ لَهُ: ارْجِعْ عَنْ دِينِكَ، فَأَبَى، فَدَعَا بِالْمِنْشَارِ فَوُضِعَ الْمِنْشَارُ فِي مَفْرِقِ رَأْسِهِ، فَشَقَّهُ حَتَّى وَقَعَ شِقَّاهُ، ثُمَّ جِيءَ بِجَلِيسِ الْمَلِكِ فقِيلَ لَهُ: ارْجِعْ عَنْ دِينِكَ فَأَبَى، فَوُضِعَ الْمِنْشَارُ فِي مَفْرِقِ رَأْسِهِ، فَشَقَّهُ بِهِ حَتَّى وَقَعَ شِقَّاهُ، ثُمَّ جِيءَ بِالْغُلَامِ فَقِيلَ لَهُ: ارْجِعْ عَنْ دِينِكَ فَأَبَى، فَدَفَعَهُ إِلَى نَفَرٍ مِنْ أَصْحَابِهِ فَقَالَ: اذْهَبُوا بِهِ إِلَى جَبَلِ كَذَا وَكَذَا فَاصْعَدُوا بِهِ الْجَبَلَ، فَإِذَا بَلَغْتُمْ ذِرْوَتَهُ فَإِنْ رَجَعَ عَنْ دِينِهِ وَإِلَّا

refused. The king then handed him over to a group of his courtiers, and said to them: 'Take him to such and such mountain; make him climb up that mountain and when you reach its peak, ask him to renounce his Faith. If he refuses to do so, push him off to his death.' So they took him and made him climb up the mountain and he said: 'O Allâh, save me from them in any way You like,' and the mountain began to shake and they all fell down (dead) and the young boy came walking to the king. The king said to him, 'What happened to your companions?' He said, 'Allâh has saved me from them.' He again handed him to some of his courtiers and said: 'Take him and carry him in a boat and when you reach the middle of the sea, ask him to renounce his religion. If he does not renounce his religion throw him (into the water).' So they took him and he said: 'O Allâh, save me from them in any way You like.' The boat turned upside down and they all drowned except the young boy who came walking to the king. The king said to him, 'What happened to your companions?' He said, 'Allâh has saved me from them.' Then he said to the king: 'You cannot kill me until you do what I command you to do.' The king asked, 'What is that?' He said, 'Gather all people in one place and tie me up to the trunk of a tree, then take an arrow

فَاطْرَحُوهُ، فَذَهَبُوا بِهِ فَصَعِدُوا بِهِ الْجَبَلَ فَقَالَ: اللَّهُمَّ اكْفِنِيهِمْ بِمَا شِئْتَ، فَرَجَفَ بِهِمُ الْجَبَلُ فَسَقَطُوا، وَجَاءَ يَمْشِي إِلَى الْمَلِكِ، فَقَالَ لَهُ الْمَلِكُ: مَا فَعَلَ أَصْحَابُكَ؟ فَقَالَ: كَفَانِيهِمُ الله تعالى، فَدَفَعَهُ إِلَى نَفَرٍ مِنْ أَصْحَابِهِ فَقَالَ: اذْهَبُوا بِهِ فَاحْمِلُوهُ فِي قُرْقُورٍ وَتَوَسَّطُوا بِهِ الْبَحْرَ، فَإِنْ رَجَعَ عَنْ دِينِهِ وَإِلَّا فَاقْذِفُوهُ، فَذَهَبُوا بِهِ فَقَالَ: اللَّهُمَّ اكْفِنِيهِمْ بِمَا شِئْتَ، فَانْكَفَأَتْ بِهِمُ السَّفِينَةُ فَغَرِقُوا، وَجَاءَ يَمْشِي إِلَى الْمَلِكِ. فَقَالَ لَهُ الْمَلِكُ: مَا فَعَلَ أَصْحَابُكَ؟ فَقَالَ: كَفَانِيهِمُ الله تَعَالَى. فَقَالَ لِلْمَلِكِ: إِنَّكَ لَسْتَ بِقَاتِلِي حَتَّى تَفْعَلَ مَا آمُرُكَ بِهِ. قَالَ: مَا هُوَ؟ قَالَ: تَجْمَعُ النَّاسَ فِي صَعِيدٍ وَاحِدٍ، وَتَصْلُبُنِي عَلَى جِذْعٍ، ثُمَّ خُذْ سَهْمًا مِنْ كِنَانَتِي، ثُمَّ ضَعِ السَّهْمَ فِي كَبِدِ الْقَوْسِ ثُمَّ قُلْ: بِسْمِ اللهِ رَبِّ الْغُلَامِ ثُمَّ ارْمِ، فَإِنَّكَ إِذَا فَعَلْتَ ذَلِكَ قَتَلْتَنِي. فَجَمَعَ النَّاسَ فِي صَعِيدٍ وَاحِدٍ، وَصَلَبَهُ عَلَى جِذْعٍ، ثُمَّ أَخَذَ سَهْمًا مِنْ

from my quiver and place the arrow in the bow and say: With the Name of Allâh, the Lord of the boy; then shoot me. If you do that you will be able to kill me.' The king called the people in an open field and tied the young boy to the trunk of a tre . He took out an arrow from his quiver, fixed it in the bow and said, 'With the Name of Allâh, the Lord of the young boy,' he then shot the arrow and it hit the boy's temple. The young boy placed his hand upon the temple where the arrow had hit him, and died. The people then said: 'We believe in the Lord of this young boy.' The king was told: 'Do you see what you were afraid of, by Allâh it has taken place; all people have believed.' The king then commanded that trenches be dug and fire lit in them, and said: 'He who would not turn back from his (the young boy's) religion, throw him in the fire' or 'he would be ordered to jump into it.' They did so till a woman came with her child. She felt hesitant in jumping into the fire. The child said to her: 'O mother! Endure (this ordeal) for you are on the Right Path.'" [*Muslim*]

كِنَانَتِهِ، ثُمَّ وَضَعَ السَّهْمَ فِي كَبِدِ الْقَوْسِ، ثُمَّ قَالَ: بِسْمِ اللهِ رَبِّ الْغُلامِ، ثُمَّ رَمَاهُ فَوَقَعَ السَّهْمُ فِي صُدْغِهِ، فَوَضَعَ يَدَهُ فِي صُدْغِهِ فَمَاتَ. فَقَالَ النَّاسُ: آمَنَّا بِرَبِّ الْغُلامِ، فَأُتِيَ الْمَلِكُ فَقِيلَ لَهُ: أَرَأَيْتَ مَا كُنْتَ تَحْذَرُ قَدْ وَاللهِ! نَزَلَ بِكَ حَذَرُكَ. قَدْ آمَنَ النَّاسُ. فَأَمَرَ بِالأُخْدُودِ بِأَفْوَاهِ السِّكَكِ فَخُدَّتْ وَأُضْرِمَ فِيهَا النِّيرَانُ وَقَالَ: مَنْ لَمْ يَرْجِعْ عَنْ دِينِهِ فَأَقْحِمُوهُ فِيهَا أَوْ قِيلَ لَهُ: اقْتَحِمْ، فَفَعَلُوا حَتَّى جَاءَتِ امْرَأَةٌ وَمَعَهَا صَبِيٌّ لَهَا، فَتَقَاعَسَتْ أَنْ تَقَعَ فِيهَا، فَقَالَ لَهَا الْغُلامُ: يَا أُمَّاهُ! اصْبِرِي فَإِنَّكِ عَلَى الْحَقِّ» رواه مسلم.

Commentary:

1. The most important lesson of this *Hadîth* is that whatever difficulties one has to face on the path of Islâm, he should endure it with patience and determination; and if the interest of Islâm requires, one should sacrifice his life for it.

2. The wonders displayed by righteous people are true. When Allâh's Will and Wisdom dictates, He manifests these wonders through His slaves.

3. It is a proof of the truth of the Qur'ân that it has retold the great historical event of

Ashâb-ul-Ukhdud (the people of the dith) which, buried in the dust of ages, had long been forgotten.

4. It is not possible to explain and interpret the Qur'ân without the help of *Ahadîth*. The event of *Ashâb-ul-Ukhdud* mentioned in the Qur'ân is an instance in point. It is the *Hadîth* that has brought into light the details of the event and clarified its ambiguity.

5. Such incidents are a source of strength for the Faith of true believers.

The Levels of *Deen* (Religion)

9. 'Umar bin Al-Khattâb رضي الله عنه said: Once we were sitting in the company of the Messenger of Allâh ﷺ when there appeared a man dressed in very white clothes and having extraordinary black hair. No signs of journey appeared on him and he was known to none of us. He sat down facing the Prophet ﷺ placing his knees against the knees of the Prophet ﷺ and placing both of his palms on his two thighs and said, "O Muhammad! Tell me about Islâm." He ﷺ replied, "Islâm is to testify that none has the right to be worshipped but Allâh, and that Muhammad is the Messenger of Allâh; that you observe *Salât* (prayers), pay *Zakât* (obligatory charity), observe *Saum* (fasting) of Ramadân and perform *Hajj* (pilgrimage) of the House, provided you have resources of making the journey to it." He replied: "You have spoken the truth." We were surprised to see that he had asked him and confirmed the correctness of

٩ - عَنْ عُمَرَ بن الخطَّابِ، رَضِيَ الله عَنْهُ، قَالَ: «بَيْنَمَا نَحْنُ جُلُوسٌ عِنْدَ رَسُولِ الله، ﷺ، ذَاتَ يَوْمٍ إِذْ طَلَعَ عَلَيْنَا رَجُلٌ شَدِيدُ بَيَاضِ الثِّيَابِ، شَدِيدُ سَوَادِ الشَّعْرِ، لَا يُرَى عَلَيْهِ أَثَرُ السَّفَرِ، وَلَا يَعْرِفُهُ مِنَّا أَحَدٌ، حَتَّى جَلَسَ إِلَى النَّبِيِّ، ﷺ، فَأَسْنَدَ رُكْبَتَيْهِ إِلَى رُكْبَتَيْهِ، وَوَضَعَ كَفَّيْهِ عَلَى فَخِذَيْهِ وقَالَ: يَا مُحَمَّدُ! أَخْبِرْنِي عَنِ الإِسْلَامِ، فقالَ رسولُ الله ﷺ: الإِسْلَامُ أَنْ تَشْهَدَ أَنْ لَا إِلٰهَ إِلَّا اللهُ، وَأَنَّ مُحَمَّدًا رَسُولُ اللهِ، وَتُقِيمَ الصَّلَاةَ، وَتُؤْتِيَ الزَّكَاةَ، وَتَصُومَ رَمَضَانَ، وَتَحُجَّ الْبَيْتَ إِنِ اسْتَطَعْتَ إِلَيْهِ سَبِيلًا. قَالَ: صَدَقْتَ. فَعَجِبْنَا لَهُ يَسْأَلُهُ وَيُصَدِّقُهُ! قَالَ: فَأَخْبِرْنِي عَنِ الإِيمَانِ. قَالَ:

the answers. He then enquired: "Tell me about *Iman*." He ﷺ said. "It is to believe in Allâh, and His Books, and His Messengers and the Last Day and that you believe in the Divine Decree, its bad and good consequences." He said, "You have spoken the truth." He then enquired: "Tell me about *Ihsân*." He ﷺ said, "It is to worship Allâh as if you are seeing Him; and although you do not see Him, He sees you." He enquired: "Inform me about the Hour (i.e., the Day of Resurrection)." He ﷺ replied, "I have no more knowledge thereof than you." He said, "Inform me about its signs." He ﷺ said, "That the servant girl gives birth to her own mistress, and that you will find the barefooted, naked, poor shepherds competing with one another in the construction of tall buildings." Then he departed. So I stayed there for a while until he ﷺ said to me, "O 'Umar! Do you know who the questioner was?" I replied, "Allâh and His Messenger know better." The Prophet ﷺ said, "He was Jibrîl (Gabriel); he has come to you all to teach you your religion." [*Muslim*]

أَنْ تُؤْمِنَ بِالله، وَمَلَائِكَتِهِ، وَكُتُبِهِ، وَرُسُلِهِ، وَالْيَوْمِ الآخِرِ، وَتُؤْمِنَ بِالْقَدَرِ خَيْرِهِ وَشَرِّهِ. قَالَ: صَدَقْتَ. قَالَ: فَأَخْبِرْنِي عَنِ الإِحْسَانِ. قَالَ: أَنْ تَعْبُدَ الله كَأَنَّكَ تَرَاهُ؛ فَإِنْ لَمْ تَكُنْ تَرَاهُ فَإِنَّهُ يَرَاكَ. قَالَ: فَأَخْبِرْنِي عَنِ السَّاعَةِ. قَالَ: مَا الْمَسْؤُولُ عَنْهَا بِأَعْلَمَ مِنَ السَّائِلِ. قَالَ: فَأَخْبِرْنِي عَنْ أَمَارَاتِهَا. قَالَ: أَنْ تَلِدَ الأَمَةُ رَبَّتَهَا، وَأَنْ تَرَى الْحُفَاةَ الْعُرَاةَ الْعَالَةَ رِعَاءَ الشَّاءِ يَتَطَاوَلُونَ فِي الْبُنْيَانِ. ثُمَّ انْطَلَقَ، فَلَبِثْتُ مَلِيًّا، ثُمَّ قَالَ: يَا عُمَرُ! أَتَدْرِي مَنِ السَّائِلُ؟ قُلْتُ: اللهُ وَرَسُولُهُ أَعْلَمُ. قَالَ: فَإِنَّهُ جِبْرِيلُ أَتَاكُمْ يُعَلِّمُكُمْ أَمْرَ دِينِكُمْ" رواه مسلم.

Commentary: This *Hadîth* is known as *Hadîth Jibrîl*. It mentions the basics of Islâm the details of which are known to every Muslim. *Al-Qadr* (Divine Decree) means that Allâh already knows and had recorded everything that will happen until the Day of Resurrection. Now whatever happens is in accordance with that knowledge and writing. What is meant by its good and bad consequences can be illustrated by saying that tranquillity, prosperity and abundance of crops come in the category of good consequences. Famine, calamities and troubles, etc., fall in the list as evil consequences. But we regard them as good or bad according to our own understanding; otherwise, every action of Allâh has some wisdom and expedience which are known to Him Alone.

Branches of *Imān*

10. Abû Hurairah رضي الله عنه: The Prophet ﷺ said, "*Imān* has some sixty or seventy branches, the best of which is the declaration that: 'None has the right to be worshipped but Allâh'; and the least of which is the removal of harmful object from the road, and modesty is a branch of *Imān*." [*Al-Bukhârî* and *Muslim*]

١٠ - عَنْ أَبِي هُرَيْرَةَ رَضِيَ الله عَنْهُ عَنِ النَّبِيِّ ﷺ قَالَ: «الإِيمَانُ بِضْعٌ وَسَبْعُونَ، أَوْ بِضْعٌ وَسِتُّونَ شُعْبَةً: فَأَفْضَلُهَا قَوْلُ لَا إِلٰهَ إِلَّا اللهُ، وَأَدْنَاهَا إِمَاطَةُ الأَذَى عَنِ الطَّرِيقِ، وَالحَيَاءُ شُعْبَةٌ مِنَ الإِيمَانِ» متفقٌ عَلَيه.

Commentary:

1. This *Hadîth* tells us that from the standpoint of practice, Faith has several stages. It also tells that Faith and practice are inseparable.
2. It also makes evident the importance and excellence of shyness because it induces a person to good deeds and deters him from evils.

The Signs of *Imān*

11. Anas bin Mâlik رضي الله عنه reported: The Prophet ﷺ said, "There are three qualities that whoever has them, will taste the sweetness of *Imān*: To love Allâh and His Messenger (ﷺ) more than anyone else; to love a person only for (the sake of) Allâh; and to abhor returning to disbelief after Allâh has saved him from it as he would abhor being thrown into the fire (of Hell)." [*Al-Bukhârî* and *Muslim*]

١١ - وَعَنْ أَنَسٍ رَضِيَ الله عَنْهُ عَنِ النَّبِيِّ ﷺ قَالَ: ثَلاثٌ مَنْ كُنَّ فِيهِ وَجَدَ بِهِنَّ حَلَاوَةَ الْإِيمَانِ: أَنْ يَكُونَ اللهُ وَرَسُولُهُ أَحَبَّ إِلَيْهِ مِمَّا سِوَاهُمَا، وَأَنْ يُحِبَّ الْمَرْءَ لا يُحِبُّهُ إِلَّا للهِ، وَأَنْ يَكْرَهَ أَنْ يَعُودَ فِي الكُفْرِ بَعْدَ أَنْ أَنْقَذَهُ اللهُ مِنْهُ، كَمَا يَكْرَهُ أَنْ يُقْذَفَ فِي النَّارِ» مَتَّفَقٌ عَلَيه.

Commentary:

1. In this *Hadîth*, the love of Allâh signifies the sweetness of *Imān*.
2. The love of Allâh and His Prophet ﷺ is the cornerstone of the Faith. When it is said that this love should exceed one's love for everything else in the universe, it means that what is enjoined by Allâh and His Prophet ﷺ must be given preference over everything else, whether it is love for the wife, children, worldly interests, desires or whims. When there is a clash between the two, the former should be given preference over the latter.

Brotherly Love and *Imān*

12. Anas رضي الله عنه reported: The Prophet ﷺ said, "No one of you becomes a true believer until he likes for his brother what he likes for himself." [*Al-Bukhârî* and *Muslim*]

١٢ - وَعَنْ أَنسٍ رَضِيَ اللهُ عَنْهُ عَنِ النَّبِيِّ ﷺ قَالَ: «لا يُؤْمِنُ أَحَدُكُمْ حَتَّى يُحِبَّ لِأَخِيهِ مَا يُحِبُّ لِنَفْسِهِ» متفقٌ عَلَيه.

Commentary: We learn from this *Hadîth* about the importance and virtue of mutual love among the Muslims. If we act upon the injunctions mentioned in this *Hadîth*, the Muslim societies will be immediately purged of the evils like exploitation, bribery, dishonesty, falsehood, cheating, forgery, etc., which are rampant in them at present. Islâm has taught golden principles to its followers who have unfortunately neglected them and in consequence are leading a life of utter disgrace and moral turpitude. May Allâh guide them to the Straight Path.

Love for the Sake of Allāh

13. Abû Hurairah رضي الله عنه reported: The Prophet ﷺ said, "A man set out to visit his brother (in Faith) in another town and Allâh sent an angel on his way. When the man met the angel, the latter asked him, "Where do you intend to go?" He said, "I intend to visit my brother in this

١٣ - وَعَنْ أَبِي هُرَيْرَةَ رَضِيَ اللهُ عَنْهُ عَنِ النَّبِيِّ ﷺ «أَنَّ رَجُلًا زَارَ أَخًا لَهُ فِي قَرْيَةٍ أُخْرَى، فَأَرْصَدَ اللهُ تَعَالَى عَلَى مَدْرَجَتِهِ مَلَكًا، فَلَمَّا أَتَى عَلَيْهِ قَالَ: أَيْنَ تُرِيدُ؟ قَالَ: أُرِيدُ أَخًا لِي فِي هٰذِهِ الْقَرْيَةِ. قَالَ: هَلْ لَكَ عَلَيْهِ

town." The angel said, "Have you done any favour to him that you intend to collect (i.e., a loan)?" He said, "No, I have no desire except to visit him because I love him for the sake of Allâh, the Exalted." Thereupon the angel said, "I am a messenger to you from Allâh (to inform you) that Allâh loves you as you love him (for His sake)." [*Muslim*]

مِنْ نِعْمَةٍ تَرُبُّهَا عَلَيْهِ؟ قَالَ: لا، غَيْرَ أَنِّي أَحْبَبْتُهُ فِي اللهِ تَعَالَى، قَالَ: فَإِنِّي رَسولُ اللهِ إِلَيْكَ بِأَنَّ اللهَ قَدْ أَحَبَّكَ كَمَا أَحْبَبْتَهُ فِيهِ» رَوَاهُ مُسْلِم.

Commentary: This *Hadîth* points out the following:

1. The great merit of visiting Muslims for Allâh's sake.
2. The bond of brotherhood in Islam is much stronger than the bonds of blood relationship and worldly interests and, therefore, comes before them in preference.
3. Whoever loves someone for Allâh's sake, Allâh will love him in a manner that suits His Majesty.

The Recognition of the Graces of Allāh

14. Abû Hurairah رضي الله عنه said that he heard the Prophet ﷺ saying: "There were three men among the Banu Isrâel, one leper, one bald and one blind. Allâh wanted to test them. He therefore, sent to them an angel who came to the leper and asked him what he would like best. He replied: 'A good colour, a good skin and to be rid of what makes me loathsome to people.' He (the angel) rubbed him and his loathsomeness vanished and he was given a good colour and a good skin. He then asked him what type of property he would like best. The leper replied that he would like camels - [or perhaps he said cattle, for Ishâq (one

١٤ - عَنْ أَبِي هُرَيْرَةَ رَضِيَ اللهُ عَنْهُ أَنَّهُ سَمِعَ النَّبِيَّ ﷺ يَقُولُ: «إِنَّ ثَلاثَةً مِنْ بَنِي إِسْرَائِيلَ: أَبْرَصَ، وَأَقْرَعَ، وَأَعْمَى، أَرَادَ اللهُ أَنْ يَبْتَلِيَهُمْ فَبَعَثَ إِلَيْهِمْ مَلَكًا، فَأَتَى الأَبْرَصَ فَقَالَ: أَيُّ شَيْءٍ أَحَبُّ إِلَيْكَ؟ قَالَ: لَوْنٌ حسنٌ، وَجِلْدٌ حَسَنٌ، وَيَذْهَبُ عَنِّي الَّذِي قَدْ قَذِرَنِي النَّاسُ؛ فَمَسَحَهُ فَذَهَبَ عَنْهُ قَذَرُهُ وَأُعْطِيَ لَوْنًا حَسَنًا. قَالَ: فَأَيُّ الْمَالِ أَحَبُّ إِلَيْكَ؟ قَالَ: الإِبِلُ - أَوْ قَالَ الْبَقَرُ - شَكَّ الرَّاوِي - فَأُعْطِيَ نَاقَةً

of the subnarrators of the *Hadîth*) was uncertain, whether he said: 'Camels,' or: 'Cattle']. He was given a pregnant she-camel and the angel invoked Allâh's Blessing on it. The angel then went to the bald man and asked him what he would like best and he replied: 'Good hair and to be rid of what makes me loathsome to people.' The angel ran his hand over him and he was given good hair. He then asked him what property he would like best. He replied that he would like cattle, so he was given a pregnant cow and the angel invoked Allâh's Blessing on it. The angel then went to the blind man and asked him what he would like best, and he replied: 'I wish that Allâh restore my sight to me so that I may see people.' Thereupon the angel ran his hand over him and Allâh restored his sight. The angel then asked what property he would like best. He replied that he would like sheep, so he was given a pregnant ewe. Flocks and herds were produced for the three men, the first having a valley full of camels, the second one, a valley full of cows and the third one a valley full of sheep. Then the angel came in the form of a leper, to the one who had been a leper, and said: 'I am a poor man and my resources have been exhausted in my journey, and my only means of reaching my destination are dependent on Allâh and then on you,

عُشَرَاءَ، فَقَالَ: بَارَكَ اللهُ لَكَ فِيهَا.

فَأَتَى الأَقْرَعَ فَقَالَ: أَيُّ شَيْءٍ أَحَبُّ إِلَيْكَ؟ قَالَ: شَعْرٌ حَسَنٌ، وَيَذْهَبُ عَنِّي هٰذَا الَّذِي قَذِرَنِي النَّاسُ، فَمَسَحَهُ فَذَهَبَ عَنْهُ وَأُعْطِيَ شَعْرًا حَسَنًا. قَالَ: فَأَيُّ الْمَالِ أَحَبُّ إِلَيْكَ؟ قَالَ: الْبَقَرُ، فَأُعْطِيَ بَقَرَةً حَامِلًا، وَقَالَ: بَارَكَ اللهُ لَكَ فِيهَا.

فَأَتَى الأَعْمَى فَقَالَ: أَيُّ شَيْءٍ أَحَبُّ إِلَيْكَ؟ قَالَ: أَنْ يَرُدَّ اللهُ إِلَيَّ بَصَرِي فَأُبْصِرَ النَّاسَ، فَمَسَحَهُ فَرَدَّ اللهُ إِلَيْهِ بَصَرَهُ. قَالَ: فَأَيُّ الْمَالِ أَحَبُّ إِلَيْكَ؟ قَالَ: الْغَنَمُ، فَأُعْطِيَ شَاةً وَالِدًا. فَأُنْتِجَ هٰذَانِ وَوَلَّدَ هٰذَا، فَكَانَ لِهٰذَا وَادٍ مِنَ الإِبِلِ، وَلِهٰذَا وَادٍ مِنَ الْبَقَرِ، وَلِهٰذَا وَادٍ مِنَ الْغَنَمِ.

ثُمَّ إِنَّهُ أَتَى الأَبْرَصَ فِي صُورَتِهِ وَهَيْئَتِهِ، فَقَالَ: رَجُلٌ مِسْكِينٌ قَدِ انْقَطَعَتْ بِيَ الْحِبَالُ فِي سَفَرِي، فَلَا بَلَاغَ لِيَ الْيَوْمَ إِلَّا بِاللهِ ثُمَّ بِكَ، أَسْأَلُكَ بِالَّذِي أَعْطَاكَ اللَّوْنَ الْحَسَنَ، وَالْجِلْدَ الْحَسَنَ، وَالْمَالَ، بَعِيرًا أَتَبَلَّغُ بِهِ فِي سَفَرِي، فَقَالَ:

الْحُقُوقُ كَثِيرَةٌ. فَقَالَ: كَأَنِّي أَعْرِفُكَ، أَلَمْ تَكُنْ أَبْرَصَ يَقْذَرُكَ النَّاسُ، فَقِيرًا فَأَعْطَاكَ اللهُ!؟ فَقَالَ: إِنَّمَا وَرِثْتُ هٰذَا المالَ كَابِرًا عَنْ كَابِرٍ، فقَالَ: إِنْ كُنْتَ كَاذِبًا فَصَيَّرَكَ اللهُ إِلَى مَا كُنْتَ.

وَأَتَى الأَقْرَعَ فِي صُورَتِهِ وَهَيْئَتِهِ، فَقَالَ لَهُ مِثْلَ مَا قَالَ لِهٰذَا، وَرَدَّ عَلَيْهِ مِثْلَ مَا رَدَّ هٰذَا، فَقَالَ: إِنْ كُنْتَ كَاذِبًا فَصَيَّرَكَ اللهُ إِلَى مَا كُنْتَ.

وَأَتَى الأَعْمَى فِي صُورَتِهِ وَهَيْئَتِهِ، فَقَالَ: رَجُلٌ مِسْكِينٌ وابْنُ سَبِيلٍ انْقَطَعَتْ بِيَ الحِبَالُ فِي سَفَرِي، فَلَا بَلاغَ لِيَ الْيَوْمَ إِلَّا بِاللهِ ثُمَّ بِكَ، أَسْأَلُكَ بالَّذِي رَدَّ عَلَيكَ بَصَرَكَ شَاةً أَتَبَلَّغُ بِهَا فِي سَفَرِي؟ فَقَالَ: قَدْ كُنْتُ أَعْمَى فَرَدَّ اللهُ إِلَيَّ بَصَرِي، فَخُذْ ما شِئْتَ وَدَعْ مَا شِئْتَ، فَوَاللهِ ما أَجْهَدُكَ الْيَوْمَ بِشَيءٍ أَخَذْتَهُ لِلّٰهِ عزَّ وَجَلَّ. فقَالَ: أَمْسِكْ مالَكَ فَإِنَّمَا ابْتُلِيتُمْ، فَقَدْ رَضِيَ الله عنكَ، وَسَخِطَ عَلَى صَاحِبَيْكَ» متفقٌ عليه.

so I ask you by Him Who gave you the good colour, the good skin and the property, for a camel by which I may get to my destination.' He replied: 'I have many dues to pay.' The angel then said: 'I think I recognize you. Were you not a leper whom people found loathsome and a poor man to whom Allâh gave property?' He replied: 'I inherited this property through generations.' The angel said: 'If you are telling a lie, may Allâh return you to your former condition.' The angel went in the form of a bald man to the one who had been bald, and said the same as he had said to the former and received a similar reply. So he said: 'If you are telling a lie, may Allâh return you to your former condition.' The angel then went to the one who had been blind and said: 'I am a poor traveller and my resources have been exhausted in my journey. My only means of reaching my destination are dependant on Allâh and then on you, so I ask you by Him Who restored your eyesight for a sheep by which I may get to the end of my journey.' He replied: 'Yes, I was blind and Allâh restored my eyesight, so take what you wish and leave what you wish. I swear by Allâh that I shall not dispute with you today concerning anything you take for Allâh's sake.' The angel said: 'Keep your property. You have all simply been put to a test, and Allâh is pleased with you and displeased with both of your companions'." [*Al-Bukhârî* and *Muslim*]

Commentary: This *Hadîth* tells us that abundance of property and wealth is also a trial. He alone succeeds in this trial who in the midst of his riches does not forget about Allâh's Status and his own status. Rather than becoming proud of his wealth, he takes pleasure in spending it in fulfilling the needs of people and expresses gratitude to Him in practical terms. Those who take an opposite course are regarded unsuccessful because on account of their wrong attitude, they tend to falsehood, pride and miserliness which cause the displeasure of Allâh.

Blessings which are often neglected

15. Ibn Abbâs رضي الله عنهما reported: The Messenger of Allâh ﷺ said, "There are two blessings in which many people incur loss. (These are) health and free time (for doing good)." [*Al-Bukhârî*]

١٥ - عَنِ ابْنِ عَبَّاسٍ رَضِيَ اللهُ عَنْهُمَا قَالَ: قَالَ رَسُولُ اللهِ ﷺ: «نِعْمَتَانِ مَغْبُونٌ فِيهِمَا كَثِيرٌ مِنَ النَّاسِ: الصِّحَّةُ، وَالْفَرَاغُ» رواه البخاري.

Commentary:

1. *Al-Ghabn* in Arabic means loss. What it really signifies is to sell something of one's own on less than its due price, or to buy something on its double or triple price. In both cases one is a loser. When a person comes to know about such a loss, he repents and feels sorry for it. This loss coupled with regret is called *Al-Ghabn*. In this *Hadîth*, man has been compared with a trader, and the health and leisure enjoyed by him to merchandise. One who uses his merchandise with care, gains profit while he who wastes it, using it carelessly, will be a loser on the Day of Resurrection.
2. The majority of people do not take proper care of both these things, with the result being that one wastes the time in useless activities and spends the physical strength and energy in the disobedience of Allâh. One will have to face severe consequences for this on the Day of Resurrection when he will be brought to account for everything.

The Believer is always Grateful

16. Abû Yahya Suhaib bin Sinân رضي الله عنه reported that the Messenger of

١٦ - وَعَنْ أَبِي يَحْيَى صُهَيْبِ بْنِ سِنَانٍ رضي الله عنه قال: قال رسول الله

Allâh ﷺ said, "How wonderful is the case of a believer; there is good for him in everything and this applies only to a believer. If prosperity befalls him, he expresses gratitude to Allâh and that is good for him; and if adversity befalls him, he endures it patiently and that is good for him." [*Muslim*]

ﷺ: «عَجَبًا لِأَمْرِ الْمُؤْمِنِ إِنَّ أَمْرَهُ كُلَّهُ لَهُ خَيْرٌ، وَلَيْسَ ذٰلِكَ لِأَحَدٍ إِلَّا لِلْمُؤْمِنِ: إِنْ أَصَابَتْهُ سَرَّاءُ شَكَرَ فَكَانَ خَيْرًا لَهُ، وَإِنْ أَصَابَتْهُ ضَرَّاءُ صَبَرَ فَكَانَ خَيْرًا لَهُ» رواه مسلم.

Commentary: A Muslim is required to behave in poverty and prosperity, affluence and hardship, in the manner stated in this *Hadîth*. It means that to forget Allâh in prosperity, rather than being thankful to Him for His Favour is defiance of His Orders. Similarly, it is unbecoming of a Muslim that in troubles and turmoil, rather than being patient, he tends to weep and cry, complaining and grieving against the Will of Allâh.

Practical Gratefulness

17. 'Âishah رضي الله عنها said: The Prophet ﷺ would stand (in prayer) at night so long that the skin of his feet would crack. I asked him, "Why do you do this of Messenger of Allâh, while your past and future sins have been forgiven?" He said, "Should I not be a grateful slave of Allâh?"

[*Al-Bukhârî* and *Muslim*]

١٧ - عَنْ عَائِشَةَ رَضِيَ اللهُ عَنْهَا أَنَّ النَّبِيَّ ﷺ كَانَ يَقُومُ مِنَ اللَّيْلِ حَتَّى تَتَفَطَّرَ قَدَمَاهُ، فَقُلْتُ لَهُ: لِمَ تَصْنَعُ هٰذَا يَا رَسُولَ اللهِ! وَقَدْ غَفَرَ اللهُ لَكَ مَا تَقَدَّمَ مِنْ ذَنْبِكَ وَمَا تَأَخَّرَ؟! قَالَ: «أَفَلَا أُحِبُّ أَنْ أَكُونَ عَبْدًا شَكُورًا؟»

Commentary:

1. All the Prophets were free from such major sins. However, some religious scholars justify some of their minor sins with plausible reasons but the majority of them maintain that they are free from all sins because of their innocence. In this situation, it does not make any sense to speak of their sins. But the fact of the matter is quite different. Anything short of excellence done by them is counted as a sin.
2. The more one is rewarded by Allâh, the greater the extent of one's gratitude to Allâh for His Benevolence should be. The best form of doing so is that one should not only be highly obedient and dutiful in the performance of the obligations but also add maximum voluntary prayers to them.

18. Narrated 'Abdullāh رَضِيَ اللهُ عَنْهُ: A man said, "O Allāh's Messenger! What is the greatest sin with Allāh?" The Prophet ﷺ said, "To set up rivals unto Allāh though He (Alone) created you." The man said, "What is next?" The Prophet ﷺ said, "To kill your son lest he should share your food with you." The man said, "What is next?" The Prophet ﷺ said, "To commit illegal sexual intercourse with the wife of your neighbour." Then Allāh revealed in confirmation of that:

"And those who invoke not any other *ilāh* (god) along with Allāh, nor kill such life as Allāh has forbidden except for just cause, nor commit illegal sexual intercourse — and whoever does this shall receive the punishment. The torment will be doubled for him..." (V.25:68,69) [*Al-Bukhāri*]

١٨ - قال عَبْدُ اللهِ: قال رَجُلٌ: يا رَسُولَ اللهِ، أيُّ الذَّنْبِ أكْبرُ عِنْدَ اللهِ تَعالَى؟ قالَ: «أنْ تَدْعُوَ للهِ نِدّاً وهُوَ خلقَكَ». قالَ: ثُمَّ أيٌّ؟ قال: «ثُمَّ أنْ تَقْتُلَ وَلَدَكَ أنْ يَطْعَمَ مَعَكَ». قال: ثُمَّ أيٌّ؟ قال: «أنْ تُزانِيَ حَليلَةَ جارِكَ»، فَأنْزَلَ اللهُ تَصْدِيقَها ﴿وَٱلَّذِينَ لَا يَدْعُونَ مَعَ ٱللَّهِ إِلَٰهًا ءَاخَرَ وَلَا يَقْتُلُونَ ٱلنَّفْسَ ٱلَّتِي حَرَّمَ ٱللَّهُ إِلَّا بِٱلْحَقِّ وَلَا يَزْنُونَ ۚ وَمَن يَفْعَلْ ذَٰلِكَ يَلْقَ أَثَامًا ﴿٦٨﴾ يُضَٰعَفْ لَهُ ٱلْعَذَابُ﴾ الآيَة.

19. Abû Bakrah Nufai' bin Al-Hârith رضي الله عنه reported: The Messenger of Allâh ﷺ said, "Shall I not inform you of the gravest of the major sins?" The Messenger of Allâh ﷺ asked this question thrice. We said, "Yes, O Messenger of Allâh. (Please inform us)." He said, "Ascribing partners with Allâh and being undutiful to your parents." The Messenger of Allâh ﷺ sat up from his reclining position and

١٩ - وَعَنْ أَبي بَكْرَةَ نُفَيْعِ بْنِ الحارِثِ رَضِيَ اللهُ عَنْهُ قَال: قالَ رَسُولُ اللهِ ﷺ: «ألا أُنَبِّئُكُمْ بِأكْبرِ الْكَبائِرِ؟» - ثَلاثاً - قُلْنا: بَلَى يا رَسُولَ اللهِ: قالَ: «الإشْراكُ بِاللهِ، وَعُقُوقُ الْوالِدَيْنِ» وَكانَ مُتَّكِئاً فَجَلَسَ، فَقالَ: «ألا وَقَوْلُ الزُّورِ وَشَهادَةُ الزُّورِ» فَما زالَ يُكَرِّرُها حَتَّى قُلْنا:

said, "And I warn you against making a false statement and a false testimony; I warn you against making a false statement and a false testimony." The Messenger of Allâh ﷺ kept on repeating that warning till we said: We wish he would stop.

[*Al-Bukhârî* and *Muslim*]

لَيْتَهُ سَكَتَ. متفقٌ عَلَيه.

Commentary: This *Hadîth* mentions some of the major sins. A major sin is one against which there is a serious warning in the Noble Qur'ân and *Hadîth*. When disobedience to parents is mentioned along with *Shirk* (polytheism), it makes the fact evident that both of these are very serious sins. Similar is the case of telling a lie and false testimony, which in the incident mentioned in this *Hadîth* made the Messenger of Allâh ﷺ leave his pillow and sit attentively. It indicates that the latter two are serious. May Allâh protect all Muslims from all such sins.

20. 'Abdullâh bin 'Amr bin Al-'Âs رضي الله عنهما reported: The Messenger of Allâh ﷺ said, "It is one of the gravest sins to abuse one's parents." It was asked (by the people): "Oh Messenger of Allâh! Can a man abuse his own parents?" The Messenger of Allâh ﷺ said, "Yes. He curses the father of somebody who in return curses his father; he then curses the mother of somebody who in return curses his mother." [*Al-Bukhârî* and *Muslim*]

Another narration states: The Messenger of Allâh ﷺ said, "One of the major sins is to curse one's parents." It was asked: "Oh Messenger of Allâh! How can a man curse his own parents?" He ﷺ said, "When someone curses the parents of another man who in return curses his

٢٠ - وَعَنْ عَبْدِالله بنِ عُمرو بن العلص رَضِيَ الله عنْهُمَا أَنَّ رَسُولَ الله ﷺ قَال: «مِن الْكَبَائِرِ شَتْمُ الرَّجُلِ وَالِدَيْهِ!» قَالُوا: يَا رَسُول الله! وَهَلْ يَشْتِمُ الرَّجُلُ وَالِدَيْهِ؟! قَال «نَعَمْ، يَسُبُّ أَبَا الرَّجُلِ، فَيَسُبُّ أَبَاهُ، وَيَسُبُّ أُمَّهُ، فَيَسُبُّ أُمَّهُ» متفقٌ عَلَيه.

وَفِي رِوَايَةٍ «إِنَّ مِنْ أَكْبَرِ الْكَبَائِرِ أَنْ يَلْعَنَ الرَّجُلُ وَالِدَيْهِ!» قِيلَ: يَا رَسُولَ اللهِ كَيْفَ يَلْعَنُ الرَّجُلُ وَالِدَيْهِ؟! قَال «يَسُبُّ أَبا الرَّجُلِ، فَيَسُبُّ أَبَاهُ، وَيَسُبُّ أُمَّهُ، فَيَسُبُّ أُمَّهُ».

father; and when someone abuses the mother of another who in return abuses his mother."

Commentary: We learn from this *Hadîth* that one should not abuse anyone's parents, because if his parents are abused in return he will be responsible for disgracing his own parents.

Signs of Hypocrites

21. Abû Hurairah رضي الله عنه reported: The Messenger of Allâh ﷺ said, "There are three signs of a hypocrite: When he speaks, he lies; when he makes a promise, he breaks it; and when he is trusted, he betrays his trust." [*Al-Bukhârî* and *Muslim*]

Another narration adds the words: "Even if he observes fasts, performs *Salât* and asserts that he is a Muslim."

٢١ - عَنْ أَبِي هُرَيْرَةَ، رَضِيَ اللهُ عَنْهُ، أَنَّ رَسُولَ اللهِ، ﷺ، قال: «آيَةُ الْمُنَافِقِ ثَلاثٌ: إِذَا حَدَّثَ كَذَبَ، وَإِذَا وَعَدَ أَخْلَفَ، وَإِذَا اؤْتُمِنَ خَانَ» متفقٌ عَليه.

وَفِي رِوَايَةٍ: «وَإِنْ صَامَ وَصَلَّى وَزَعَمَ أَنَّهُ مُسْلِمٌ».

Commentary: A hypocrite is the one who professes Islâm before the Muslims but conceals hatred and animosity against them. This double-dealing is worse than *Kufr*. This is the reason the Noble Qur'ân has declared about them that they will be in the lowest depths of the Hell. The hypocrites referred to here lived at the time of the Prophet ﷺ and he was informed about them through *Wahy* (Revelation). It is very difficult to identify this class of hypocrites in this age. It is almost impossible to know the hypocrisy of Faith. The practical hypocrisy is, however, now very common among the Muslims. It can be identified by the traits which have been stated in the *Ahâdîth* about them. These traits are very common among many of the present-day Muslims. Their conduct bears the marks of hypocrisy. This practical hypocrisy is, however, not *Kufr* as is the case with the hypocrisy of Faith.

Yawning is from Shaitan

22. Abû Hurairah رضي الله عنه

٢٢ - عَنْ أَبِي هُرَيْرَةَ رَضِيَ اللهُ عَنْهُ أَنَّ

reported: The Prophet ﷺ said, "Allâh likes sneezing and dislikes yawning. When any one of you sneezes and says '*Al-hamdu lillâh* (praise be to Allâh)', it becomes obligatory upon every Muslim who hears him to respond with '*Yarhamuk-Allâh* (may Allâh have mercy on you)'. Yawning is from the devil. When one of you feels like yawning, he should restrain it as much as possible, for the devil laughs at you when one of you yawns." [*Al-Bukhârî*]

النَّبِيَّ ﷺ قَالَ: «إِنَّ اللهَ يُحِبُّ الْعُطَاسَ، وَيَكْرَهُ التَّثَاؤُبَ، فَإِذَا عَطَسَ أَحَدُكُمْ وَحَمِدَ اللهَ تَعَالَى كَانَ حَقًّا عَلَى كُلِّ مُسْلِمٍ سَمِعَهُ أَنْ يَقُولَ لَهُ: يَرْحَمُكَ اللهُ، وَأَمَّا التَّثَاؤُبُ فَإِنَّمَا هُوَ مِنَ الشَّيْطَانِ، فَإِذَا تَثَاءَبَ أَحَدُكُمْ فَلْيَرُدَّهُ مَا اسْتَطَاعَ؛ فَإِنَّ أَحَدَكُمْ إِذَا تَثَاءَبَ ضَحِكَ مِنْهُ الشَّيْطَانُ» رَوَاهُ الْبُخَارِي.

Commentary: Sneezing lightens the mind of man, and makes him feels comfort in his body. It is therefore something good and one should glorify Allâh for it. However, yawning is indicative of gluttony, sloth and heaviness and is considered disagreeable. The Prophet ﷺ commanded us to stop it either by closing our mouth or by putting our hand across it in order to avoid an act which pleases Satan.

23. Abû Sa'îd Al-Khudrî رضي الله عنه reported: The Messenger of Allâh ﷺ said, "When one yawns, he should put his hand over his mouth, otherwise the devil will enter." [*Muslim*]

٢٣ - وَعَنْ أَبِي سعيدٍ الْخُدْرِيِّ رَضِيَ اللهُ عَنْهُ قَال: قَالَ رَسُولُ اللهِ ﷺ: «إِذَا تَثَاءَبَ أَحَدُكُمْ فَلْيُمْسِكْ بِيَدِهِ عَلَى فِيهِ، فَإِنَّ الشَّيْطَانَ يَدْخُلُ» رَوَاهُ مُسلم

Commentary: At the time of yawning one should put his hand across his mouth. It is a disliked act or *Makrûh* to yawn noisily, because this act pleases Satan. In other words, we must not miss any chance to degrade and frustrate Satan.

Keeping *Shaitān* away

24. Jâbir رضي الله عنه reported: I heard the Messenger of Allâh ﷺ saying, "If a person mentions the Name of Allâh upon entering his house and eating,

٢٤ - وَعَنْ جَابِرٍ، رَضِيَ اللهُ عَنْهُ قَال: سَمِعْتُ رَسُولَ اللهِ ﷺ يَقُولُ: «إِذَا دَخَلَ الرَّجُلُ بَيْتَهُ، فَذَكَرَ اللهَ تَعَالَى

Satan says, addressing his followers: 'You will find no where to spend the night and no dinner (here).' But if he enters without mentioning the Name of Allâh, Satan says (to his followers): 'You have found (a place) to spend the night,' and if he does not mention the Name of Allâh at the time of eating, Satan says: 'You have found (a place) to spend the night as well as food.'" [*Muslim*]

عِنْدَ دُخُولِهِ وَعِنْدَ طَعَامِهِ، قَالَ الشَّيْطَانُ لِأَصْحَابِهِ: لَا مَبِيتَ لَكُمْ وَلَا عَشَاءَ، وَإِذَا دَخَلَ، فَلَمْ يَذْكُرِ اللهَ تَعَالَى عِنْدَ دُخُولِهِ، قَالَ الشَّيْطَانُ: أَدْرَكْتُمُ الْمَبِيتَ، وَإِذَا لَمْ يَذْكُرِ اللهَ تَعَالَى عِنْدَ طَعَامِهِ قَالَ: أَدْرَكْتُمُ الْمَبِيتَ وَالْعَشَاءَ» رَوَاهُ مُسلم.

Commentary: Here, we are told that in order to ward off Satan and his followers, we are supposed to remember Allâh before entering our house and before beginning to eat. The remembrance of Allâh implies those appropriate prayers of the Prophet ﷺ which have been mentioned in *Ahâdith*. For example, we are instructed to pronounce the Name of Allâh before beginning to eat. On entering our house we recite the following Prophetic prayer: "*Allâhumma inni as'aluka khairal-mawliji wa khairal-makhraji. Bismillâhi walajnâ, wa bismillâhi kharajnâ, wa 'al-Allâhi rabbinâ tawakkalnâ.*" (O Allâh! I ask you for what is good of entrance and what is good for an exit. With the Name of Allâh do we enter, and with the Name of Allâh do we leave, and upon our Lord Allâh have we put our trust.)

Wudhu' (Ablution) washes off Sins

25. Abû Hurairah رضي الله عنه reported: The Messenger of Allâh ﷺ said, "When a servant (of Allâh) Muslim or a believer washes his face (in the course of *Wudhu'*), every sin he has committed with his eyes is washed away from his face along with the water, or with the last drop of water; when he washes his hands, every sin they wrought is erased from his hands with the water, or with the last drop of water; and when he washes his feet,

٢٥ - عَنْ أَبِي هُرَيْرَةَ رَضِيَ اللهُ عَنْهُ أَنَّ رَسُولَ اللهِ ﷺ قَالَ: «إِذَا تَوَضَّأَ الْعَبْدُ الْمُسْلِمُ، أَوِ الْمُؤْمِنُ فَغَسَلَ وَجْهَهُ خَرَجَ مِنْ وَجْهِهِ كُلُّ خَطِيئَةٍ نَظَرَ إِلَيْهَا بِعَيْنَيْهِ مَعَ الْمَاءِ، أَوْ مَعَ آخِرِ قَطْرِ الْمَاءِ، فَإِذَا غَسَلَ يَدَيْهِ خَرَجَ مِنْ يَدَيْهِ كُلُّ خَطِيئَةٍ كَانَ بَطَشَتْهَا يَدَاهُ مَعَ الْمَاءِ، أَوْ مَعَ آخِرِ قَطْرِ الْمَاءِ فَإِذَا

every sin towards which his feet walked is washed away with water, or with the last drop of water, with the result that he comes out cleansed of all sins." [*Muslim*]

غسَلَ رِجْلَيْهِ خَرَجَتْ كُلُّ خَطِيئَةٍ مَشَتْهَا رِجْلَاهُ مَعَ الْمَاءِ أَوْ مَعَ آخِرِ قَطْرِ الْمَاءِ حَتَّى يَخْرُجَ نَقِيًّا مِنَ الذُّنُوبِ» رَوَاهُ مسلم.

Commentary: This *Hadîth* mentions the excellence of *Wudhu'*. Obviously a person who performs *Wudhu'* five times daily would be free from sins. Thus, *Wudhu'* is a means of both outward and inward cleanliness.

How to proceed to *Salāt*

26. Abû Hurairah رضي الله عنه reported: I heard the Messenger of Allâh ﷺ saying, "When the *Iqâmah* is pronounced, do not come to it running. Rather, you should walk calmly with tranquillity to join the congregation. Then pray what you catch and complete what you miss."
[*Al-Bukhârî* and *Muslim*]

In *Muslim* it is added: The Messenger of Allâh ﷺ said, "For when one of you is walking to the *Salât*, he is actually engaged in *Salât*."

٢٦ - وَعَنْ أَبِي هُرَيْرَةَ رَضِيَ اللهُ عَنْهُ قَالَ: سَمِعْتُ رَسُولَ اللهِ ﷺ يَقُولُ: «إِذَا أُقِيمَتِ الصَّلاةُ، فَلا تَأْتُوهَا وَأَنْتُمْ تَسْعَوْنَ، وَأْتُوهَا وَأَنْتُمْ تَمْشُونَ، وَعَلَيْكُمُ السَّكِينَةُ، فَمَا أَدْرَكْتُمْ فَصَلُّوا، وَمَا فَاتَكُمْ فَأَتِمُّوا» متفقٌ عليه.

زَادَ مسلم في رِوَايَةٍ له: «فَإِنَّ أَحَدَكُمْ إِذَا كَانَ يَعْمِدُ إِلَى الصَّلاةِ فَهُوَ فِي صَلاةٍ».

Commentary: This *Hadîth* prevents us from running or walking hurriedly in order to join a congregational prayer because this is undignified. Whereas, we are commanded to be self-composed and dignified with regard to all matters. Secondly, when a believer walks to the mosque after performing ablution at home, he is considered to be in a state of *Salât*. Thirdly, the first *Rak'ah* he prays behind the *Imâm* will be counted as his first *Rak'ah*, so he must make up for the *Rak'ahs* he may have missed, if any, after the *Imâm* has concluded his *Salât*.

27. Abû Hurairah رضي الله عنه reported: The Prophet ﷺ said, "He

٢٧ - عَنْ أَبِي هُرَيْرَةَ رَضِيَ اللهُ عَنْهُ أَنَّ النَّبِيَّ ﷺ قَالَ: «مَنْ غَدَا إِلَى

who goes to the mosque in the morning or in the evening, Allâh prepares for him a place in *Jannah* whenever he goes to the mosque in the morning or the evening." [*Al-Bukhârî* and *Muslim*]

الْمَسْجِدِ أَوْ رَاحَ، أَعَدَّ اللهُ لَهُ فِي الْجَنَّةِ نُزُلًا كُلَّمَا غَدَا أَوْ رَاحَ» متفقٌ عَلَيه.

Commentary: This *Hadîth* points out the merit of going on foot to the mosque for *Salât*, no matter whether one goes in the morning or the evening. In fact, the heart of a Muslim should be attached to mosques and on account of this he should go there at all the prescribed hours of *Salât* to perform his *Salât* in congregation.

28. Abû Hurairah رضي الله عنه reported: The Prophet ﷺ said, "He who purifies himself (performs *Wudhu'*) in his house and then walks to one of the houses of Allâh (mosque) for performing an obligatory *Salât*, one step of his will wipe out his sins and another step will elevate his rank (in *Jannah*)." [*Muslim*]

٢٨- وَعَنْ أَبِي هُرَيْرَةَ رَضِيَ اللهُ عَنْهُ أَنَّ النَّبِيَّ ﷺ قَالَ: «مَنْ تَطَهَّرَ فِي بَيْتِهِ، ثُمَّ مَضَى إِلَى بَيْتٍ مِنْ بُيُوتِ اللهِ؛ لِيَقْضِيَ فَرِيضَةً مِنْ فَرَائِضِ اللهِ، كَانَتْ خُطُوَاتُهُ، إِحْدَاهَا تَحُطُّ خَطِيئَةً، وَالأُخْرَى تَرْفَعُ دَرَجَةً» رَوَاهُ مسلم.

Commentary: This *Hadîth* has an inducement for offering *Salât* in the mosque and explains the merit of doing so. The merit lies in the fact that one minor sin is pardoned with every step that is taken towards the mosque and one's status (in *Jannah*) is enhanced by one degree. This *Hadîth* also mentions the vastness of the Mercy and Blessing of Allâh.

Sitting in the Mosque

29. Jâbir bin Samurah رضي الله عنه reported: After the *Fajr* (dawn) prayer the Prophet ﷺ used to sit crossed legged in the same place (in which he had prayed) till the sun had brightly risen. [*Abû Dâwûd* and others with authentic chains of narration.]

٢٩ - وَعَنْ جَابِرِ بن سَمُرَةَ رَضِيَ اللهُ عَنْهُ قَال: كَانَ النَّبِيُّ ﷺ إِذَا صَلَّى الْفَجْرَ تَرَبَّعَ فِي مَجْلِسِهِ حَتَّى تَطْلُعَ الشَّمْسُ حَسْنَاءَ. حَدِيثٌ صَحِيحٌ، رَوَاهُ أَبُو دَاود وغيره بِأَسَانِيدَ صَحِيحَةٍ.

Commentary: This *Hadîth* tells us that it is commendable to stay in the mosque after offering *Fajr* prayer with the congregation until sunrise. It also commends sitting cross-legged.

Excellence of the *Fajr* and *'Asr* Prayers

30. Abû Hurairah رضـي الله عـنـه reported: The Messenger of Allâh ﷺ said, "There are angels who take turns in visiting you by night and by day, and they all assemble at the dawn (*Fajr*) and the afternoon (*'Asr*) prayers. Those who have spent the night with you, ascend (to the heaven) and Allâh, Who knows better about them, asks: 'In what condition did you leave My slaves?' They reply: 'We left them while they were performing *Salât* and we went to them while they were performing *Salât*.'" [*Al-Bukhârî* and *Muslim*]

٣٠ - وَعَنْ أَبِي هُرَيْرَةَ رَضِيَ اللهُ عَنْهُ قَالَ: قَالَ رَسُولُ اللهِ ﷺ: «يَتَعَاقَبُونَ فِيكُم مَلائِكَةٌ بِاللَّيْلِ، وَمَلائِكَةٌ بِالنَّهَارِ، وَيَجْتَمِعُونَ فِي صَلَاةِ الصُّبْحِ وَصَلَاةِ الْعَصْرِ، ثُمَّ يَعْرُجُ الَّذِينَ بَاتُوا فِيكُم، فَيَسْأَلُهُمُ اللهُ - وَهُوَ أَعْلَمُ بِهِمْ - كَيْفَ تَرَكْتُمْ عِبَادِي؟ فَيَقُولُونَ: تَرَكْنَاهُمْ وَهُمْ يُصَلُّونَ، وَأَتَيْنَاهُمْ وَهُمْ يُصَلُّونَ» متفقٌ عليه.

Commentary: The angels for the night come at the time of *'Asr* when the angels for the morning are present. This is how the angels of the two shifts assemble at this time. The angels of the shift of *'Asr* leave their duty in the morning, and the angels of the morning shift resume their duty when the pious persons are engaged in *Fajr* prayer. This is how the two groups assemble again at that time. Thus, when the angels come or go, the people who are punctual in their prayer are engaged in *Fajr* and *'Asr*. Almighty Allâh knows everything but even then He asks the angels about his pious slaves so that the piousness of the believers and their merit and distinction become evident to them.

When to teach Children *Salāt*

31. Sabrah bin Ma'bad Al-Juhanî رضي الله عنه reported: The Messenger of Allâh ﷺ said, "Teach a boy *Salât* (the prayer) when he attains the age of

٣١ - وَعَنْ أَبِي ثُرَيَّةَ سَبْرَةَ بنِ مَعْبَدٍ الْجُهَنِيِّ رَضِيَ اللهُ عَنْهُ قَالَ: قَالَ رَسُولُ اللهِ ﷺ: «عَلِّمُوا الصَّبِيَّ الصَّلَاةَ

seven years, and punish him (if he does not offer it) at ten." [*Abû Dâwûd* and *At-Tirmidhi* who said it is a good *Hadith*]

لِسَبْعِ سِنِينَ» وَاضْرِبُوهُ عَلَيْهَا ابْنَ عَشْرِ سِنِينَ» حَدِيثٌ حَسَنٌ رَوَاهُ أَبُو دَاود، والتِّرْمِذِيُّ. وَقَال: حَدِيثٌ حَسَنٌ.

The narration in *Abû Dâwûd* states: The Messenger of Allâh ﷺ said, "Order a boy to perform *Salât* (the prayer) when he is seven years old."

وَلَفْظُ أَبِي دَاوُدَ: «مُرُوا الصَّبِيَّ بِالصَّلاَةِ إِذَا بَلَغَ سَبْعَ سِنِينَ».

Commentary: Obviously only such teachers and parents can persuade the children to perform *Salât* who are themselves very strict about it. In the early period of Islâm, one could not even think of a Muslim who ignored it. It is very unfortunate indeed that in the present-day Muslim societies, a large majority of Muslims are careless about this fundamental religious duty. In such a state of affairs who would instruct and persuade them to perform this major religious obligation?

The Value of *Dhikr*

32. Narrated Abū Hurairah رَضِيَ اللهُ عَنْهُ: The Prophet ﷺ said, "(There are) two expressions (sayings) which are dear to the Most Gracious (Allāh) and very easy for the tongue to say, but very heavy in weight in the balance. These are:

'Subḥān Allāhi wa biḥamdihī' and *'Subḥān Allāhil–'Adhīm'*." (Glory to Allâh and praise be to Him, and glory to Allâh The Most Great) [*Al-Bukhāri*]

٣٢ - عن أبي هُرَيْرَةَ رَضِيَ اللهُ عَنْهُ قَالَ: قال النَّبِيُّ ﷺ: «كلِمَتانِ حَبيبَتانِ إلى الرَّحْمٰنِ، خَفيفَتانِ عَلى اللِّسانِ، ثَقيلَتانِ في المِيزانِ: سُبْحانَ اللهِ وبِحَمْدِهِ، سُبْحانَ اللهِ العَظِيمِ».

Remembering Allāh at all Times

33. Abû Hurairah رضي الله عنه reported: The Messenger of Allâh ﷺ said, "If anyone sits in a gathering where he does not remember Allâh, he will bring grief upon himself from

٣٣ - وَعَنْ أَبِي هُرَيْرَةَ رَضِيَ الله عَنْهُ عَنْ رَسُولِ الله ﷺ قَال: «مَنْ قَعَدَ مَقْعَدًا لَم يذكرِ الله تَعَالَى فِيهِ كَانَتْ عَلَيهِ مِنَ الله تِرَةٌ، وَمَن اضطَجَعَ

Allâh (on the Day of Resurrection), and he who lies down in a place where he does not remember Allâh, will bring grief upon himself from Allâh (on the Day of Resurrection)." [*Abû Dâwûd*]

مَضْجَعًا لَا يَذْكُرُ اللهَ تَعَالَى فِيهِ كَانَتْ عَلَيْهِ مِنَ اللهِ تِرَةٌ» رَوَاهُ أَبُو داود. وَقَدْ سَبَقَ قَرِيبًا وَشَرَحْنَا «التِّرَةَ» فِيهِ.

Commentary: Man should remember Allâh on all occasions. This will establish and cement his bond with Allâh, keeping heedlessness away from his heart and mind. It is heedlessness which prompts man to transgress Divine rules and limits, whereas the remembrance of Allâh prevents him from indulging in backbiting and passing slanderous remarks against people in their absence or reproaching and belittling someone at a meeting. Unfortunately, such petty and negative out-pourings are relished at chat sessions in our society. This generates grudge, ill-will and hostility in hearts and splits up social cohesion and Islâmic solidarity. Every Muslim should therefore take care to avoid such gatherings.

Seeking Forgiveness Daily

34. Al-Agharr bin Yasâr Al-Muzani رضي الله عنه narrated that the Messenger of Allâh ﷺ said, "Turn you people in repentance to Allâh and seek His Forgiveness. I turn to Him in repentance a hundred times a day." [*Muslim*]

٣٤ - وَعَنِ الأَغَرِّ بْنِ يَسَارٍ المُزَنِيِّ رضي الله عنه قال: قال رسول الله ﷺ: «يا أَيُّهَا النَّاسُ! تُوبُوا إِلى اللهِ واسْتَغْفِرُوهُ فإِنِّي أَتُوبُ في الْيَوْمِ مِائَةَ مَرَّةٍ» رواه مسلم.

The Importance of Greeting

35. Abdullâh bin 'Amr bin Al-'Âs رضي الله عنهما reported: A man asked the Messenger of Allâh ﷺ: "Which act in Islâm is the best?" He ﷺ replied, "To give food, and to greet those who you know and those you do not know." [*Al-Bukhârî* and *Muslim*]

٣٥ - وَعَنْ عَبدِ اللهِ بنِ عمرو بن الْعَاص رَضِيَ اللهُ عَنْهُمَا أَنَّ رَجُلًا سَأَلَ رَسُولَ اللهِ ﷺ: أَيُّ الإِسْلامِ خَيْرٌ؟ قَال: «تُطْعِمُ الطَّعَامَ، وَتَقْرَأُ السَّلامَ عَلى مَنْ عَرَفْتَ وَمَنْ لَمْ تَعْرِف» متفقٌ عَلَيه.

Commentary: Feeding the poor and destitute is an act of goodness, and so is fulfilling the needs of the indigent. Greeting everybody (saying *'As-Salâmu 'Alaikum'*), whether an acquaintance or a stranger, is a good manner too. Both of these acts generate mutual love and remove hatred and ill-will from hearts. All other forms of greetings do not substitute for the Islâmic greeting.

36. Abû Hurairah رضي الله عنه reported: The Messenger of Allâh ﷺ said, "You will not enter *Jannah* until you believe, and you will not believe until you love one another. Shall I inform you of something which, if you do, you will love one another? Promote greetings amongst yourselves." [*Muslim*]

٣٦- وَعَنْ أَبِي هُرَيْرَةَ رَضِيَ اللهُ عَنْهُ قَالَ: قَالَ رَسُولُ اللهِ ﷺ: «لَا تَدْخُلُوا الْجَنَّةَ حَتَّى تُؤْمِنُوا، وَلَا تُؤْمِنُوا حَتَّى تَحَابُّوا، أَوَلَا أَدُلُّكُمْ عَلَى شَيْءٍ إِذَا فَعَلْتُمُوهُ تَحَابَبْتُمْ؟ أَفْشُوا السَّلَامَ بَيْنَكُمْ» رَوَاهُ مسلم.

Commentary: Imān is a prerequisite for entry to *Jannah*. Whereas mutual love among Muslims is complementary to it, and this quality can only be attained by giving a social character to the Islâmic form of greeting; that is to say, *'As-Salâmu 'Alaikum*.

Winning the Love of Allāh

37. Sahl bin Sa'd As-Sâ'idî رضي الله عنه reported: A man came to the Prophet ﷺ and said, "O Messenger of Allâh, guide me to such an action which if I do it Allâh will love me and the people will also love me." He ﷺ said, "Have no desire for this world, Allâh will love you; and have no desire for what people possess, people will love you." [*Ibn Mâjah* and others. Some consider it good and Albâni said it is authentic in As-Sahihah. However, Muqbil Al-Wâdi'i and Mustafâ Al-'Adawi consid-

٣٧ - وَعَنْ سَهْلِ بنِ سَعْدٍ السَّاعِدِيِّ، رَضِيَ اللهُ عَنْهُ، قَالَ: جَاءَ رَجُلٌ إِلَى النَّبِيِّ ﷺ، فَقَالَ: يَا رَسُولَ اللهِ دُلَّنِي عَلَى عَمَلٍ إِذَا عَمِلْتُهُ أَحَبَّنِي اللهُ، وَأَحَبَّنِي النَّاسُ، فَقَالَ: «ازْهَدْ فِي الدُّنْيَا يُحِبَّكَ اللهُ، وَازْهَدْ فِيمَا عِنْدَ النَّاسِ يُحِبَّكَ النَّاسُ» حَدِيثٌ حَسَنٌ رَوَاهُ ابن مَاجَه وَغَيْرُه بِأَسَانِيدَ حَسَنَةٍ.

er it unauthentic.]

Commentary: *Zuhd* (ascetism) does not mean renunciation of the world and obligations of life. What it really means is that one should be contented with what he possesses and rids himself of greed. Islâm neither permits renunciation of the world nor does it condemn genuine struggle to acquire wealth and riches. Therefore, involvement in worldly affairs and struggle for lawful means of livelihood are not against *Zuhd*. A person who is contented with the lawful means of income is a distinguished person as all his activities are exalted to the level of worship. Similarly, unconcern with the wealth and riches of others and ignoring them is a part of *Zuhd* and contentment. One additional advantage of it is that such a person wins the love and respect of the people because he who begs people, rather than Allâh, has to suffer disgrace and is disliked by the people. The case of begging from Allâh is just the opposite. The more a person begs Him, the more pleased He will be with him. In fact, He is displeased if someone does not beg Him. This has been exquisitely stated in an Arabic verse of poetry the meaning of which is:

"Do not stretch your hands before anyone for your needs, but beg from Him (Allâh) whose door is always open."

"If a person does not beg Him (Allâh), He is displeased, while if one begs someone He becomes furious."

Arrogance bars from Allāh

38. 'Abdullâh bin Mas'ud رضي الله عنه reported: The Prophet ﷺ said, "He who has in his heart an ant's weight of arrogance will not enter *Jannah*." Someone said: "A man likes to wear beautiful clothes and shoes?" The Prophet ﷺ said, "Allâh is Beautiful and He loves beauty. Arrogance means ridiculing and rejecting the Truth and despising people." [*Muslim*]

٣٨ - وَعَنْ عَبْدِ الله بن مَسْعُودٍ رَضِيَ الله عَنْهُ، عَنِ النَّبِيِّ ﷺ قَال: «لَا يَدْخُلُ الْجَنَّةَ مَنْ كَانَ فِي قَلْبِهِ مِثْقَالُ ذَرَّةٍ مِنْ كِبْرٍ» فَقَالَ رَجُلٌ: إِنَّ الرَّجُلَ يُحِبُّ أَنْ يَكُونَ ثَوْبُهُ حَسَنًا، وَنَعْلُهُ حَسَنَةً؟ قَالَ: «إِنَّ الله جَمِيلٌ يُحِبُّ الْجَمَالَ، الْكِبْرُ بَطَرُ الْحَقِّ وَغَمْطُ النَّاسِ» رَوَاهُ مُسْلِم.

Commentary: The *Hadîth* says that a man who has even an iota of pride in his heart will be barred from entering *Jannah*. The word *Dharrah* used for the smallest amount means in Arabic either the smallest ant or the particle which is radiated by sun-rays and seen through a whole in the wall. Obviously, such a particle has almost a non-existent amount, but even this much is disapproved by Allâh. If pride incites a man to deny the existence of Allâh and His Revelation, he is sure to be thrown into Hell. He also faces Divine displeasure and the danger of infernal fire if mere consideration of riches, physical beauty, social and intellectual prominence and family status makes him proud and self-conceited and he looks down upon others, or persists in the denial of Truth. First he will receive punishment and only after that will he be admitted into *Jannah*. Good dress, however, is not considered the sign of pride.

Never belittle a Good Deed

39. Abû Dharr رضي الله عنه reported: The Prophet ﷺ said to me, "Do not belittle any good deed, even your meeting with your brother (Muslim) with a cheerful face." [*Muslim*]

٣٩ - عَنْ أَبِي ذر رَضِيَ اللهُ عَنْهُ : قَالَ لِي النَّبِيُّ ﷺ: «لَا تَحْقِرَنَّ مِنَ الْمَعْرُوفِ شَيْئًا وَلَوْ أَنْ تَلْقَى أَخَاكَ بِوَجْهٍ طَلِيقٍ» رَواه مسلم.

Commentary: Every deed approved by the *Sharī'ah* is considered good and rewarding. No matter how seemingly small people may consider it, it must not be looked at from a highbrow angle. Even to meet people cheerfully is one of the Islamic virtues, though it may appear quite insignificant to some people.

Refraining from the Doubtful

40. An-Nu'mân bin Bashîr رضي الله عنهما heard the Messenger of Allâh ﷺ say, "What is lawful is clear and what is unlawful is clear, but between them are certain doubtful things which many people do not know. So he who guards against doubtful things keeps his religion and his honor blameless. But he who falls into doubtful things falls into that which is unlawful, just as

٤٠ - وَعَنِ النُّعْمَانِ بنِ بَشِيرٍ رَضِيَ اللهُ عَنْهُمَا قَال: سَمِعْتُ رَسُولَ اللهِ ﷺ يَقُولُ: «إِنَّ الْحَلَالَ بَيِّنٌ، وَإِنَّ الْحَرَامَ بَيِّنٌ، وَبَيْنَهُمَا مُشْتَبِهَاتٌ لا يَعْلَمُهُنَّ كَثِيرٌ مِنَ النَّاسِ، فَمَنِ اتَّقَى الشُّبُهَاتِ، اسْتَبْرَأَ لِدِينِهِ وَعِرْضِهِ، وَمَنْ وَقَعَ فِي الشُّبُهَاتِ، وَقَعَ فِي

a shepherd who grazes his cattle in the vicinity of a pasture declared prohibited (by the king); he is likely to stray into the pasture. Mind you, every king has a protected pasture and Allâh's protected pasture is that which He has declared unlawful. Verily, there is a piece of flesh in the body, if it is healthy, the whole body is healthy, and if it is corrupt, the whole body is corrupt. Verily, it is the heart." [*Al-Bukhârî* and *Muslim*]

الْحَرَامِ، كَالرَّاعِي يَرْعَى حَوْلَ الحِمَى يُوشِكُ أَنْ يَرْتَعَ فِيهِ، أَلا! وَإِنَّ لِكُلِّ مَلِكٍ حِمىً، أَلا! وَإِنَّ حِمَى اللهِ مَحَارِمُهُ، أَلا! وَإِنَّ فِي الْجَسَدِ مُضْغَةً إِذَا صَلَحَتْ صَلَحَ الْجَسَدُ كُلُّهُ، وَإِذَا فَسَدَتْ فَسَدَ الْجَسَدُ كُلُّهُ: أَلا! وَهِيَ الْقَلْبُ» متفقٌ عَليه. وَرَوَيَاهُ مِنْ طُرُقٍ بِأَلْفَاظٍ مُتَقَارِبَةٍ.

Commentary: There are such meeting-points between what is permissible and what is not permissible in the matter of religion of which the majority of people are ignorant. If man abstains from them, it means that he is keeping his duty to Allâh. Yet, if he is involved in them without caring for what is allowable or unallowable, he may overstep the Divine limits. Businessmen and traders are particularly warned here to avoid things of a dubious nature and are urged to adopt only that pattern which is lawful. Another important point underlying this *Hadîth* concerns the heart. Its purity or impurity directly affects the human conduct in a good or bad way. Therefore, it is absolutely necessary to cleanse the heart of all evils and impurities, and this is not possible without sound Faith and consciousness of Allâh.

41. An-Nawwâs bin Sam'ân رضي الله عنه reported: The Prophet ﷺ said, "Piety is good manners, and sin is that which creates doubt in your heart and you do not like people to know of it." [*Muslim*]

٤١ - وَعَنِ النَّوَّاسِ بنِ سَمعانَ رَضِيَ اللهُ عَنْهُ عَنِ النَّبِيِّ ﷺ قَال: «الْبِرُّ حُسنُ الْخُلُقِ، وَالإِثمُ مَا حَاكَ فِي نَفْسِكَ، وَكَرِهْتَ أَنْ يَطَّلِعَ عَلَيْهِ النَّاسُ» رَوَاهُ مسلم.

«حَاكَ» بِالْحَاءِ الْمُهْمَلَةِ وَالْكَافِ، أَيْ: تَرَدَّدَ فِيهِ.

Commentary: Islâm lays much importance on courteous behaviour and also explains and stresses its different aspects. To meet people cheerfully, to avoid causing trouble to them, to try to make things convenient and comfortable for them, to do social service, to extend co-operation to others in good things and to be generous, and to like for others what you like for yourself, are all forms of moral behaviour that are counted as virtues in Islâm. All that is bad and vicious is considered by Islâm as sinful. This *Hadîth* describes two signs of a sin. First, man should feel guilt in committing it. Second, one does not like others being informed about it. The *Hadîth* further tells us that human nature leads man to correct conclusions and keeps him away from evils, provided it has not been deformed by the environment and bad company.

42. Hasan bin 'Ali رضي الله عنهما said: I remember (these words) from Messenger of Allâh ﷺ: "Give up what is doubtful to you for that which is not doubtful." [*At-Tirmidhî* and he graded it good and authentic.]

٤٢ - وَعَنِ الْحَسَنِ بن عَلِيٍّ رَضِيَ اللهُ عَنْهُمَا، قَالَ: حَفِظْتُ مِنْ رَسُولِ اللهِ ﷺ: «دَعْ مَا يَرِيبُكَ إِلَى مَا لَا يَرِيبُكَ» رَوَاهُ التِّرْمِذِيُّ وَقَالَ: حَدِيثٌ حَسَنٌ صَحِيحٌ.

مَعْنَاهُ: اتْرُكْ مَا تَشُكُّ فِيهِ، وَخُذْ مَا لَا تَشُكُّ فِيهِ.

Commentary: This *Hadîth* leads us to the conclusion that one must always avoid doubtful things so that he does not do anything unlawful. This message is repeated in another *Hadîth* which says that he who has saved himself from doubts has in fact saved his Faith and honour.

Rewards for helping Animals

43. Abû Hurairah رضي الله عنه reported: The Messenger of Allâh ﷺ said, "While a man was walking on his way he became extremely thirsty. He found a well, so he went down into it to drink water and then he came out. Upon leaving it, he saw a dog which was panting due to thirst. His tongue was lolling out and he was eating moist earth from extreme thirst. The man thought to himself: 'This dog is extremely thirsty as I was.' So he descended into the well, filled up his

٤٣ - عَنْ أَبِي هُرَيْرَةَ رَضِيَ اللهُ عَنْهُ أَنَّ رَسُولَ اللهِ ﷺ قَالَ: «بَيْنَمَا رَجُلٌ يَمْشِي بِطَرِيقٍ اشْتَدَّ عَلَيْهِ الْعَطَشُ، فَوَجَدَ بِئْرًا فَنَزَلَ فِيهَا فَشَرِبَ ثُمَّ خَرَجَ، فَإِذَا كَلْبٌ يَلْهَثُ يَأْكُلُ الثَّرَى مِنَ الْعَطَشِ، فَقَالَ الرَّجُلُ: لَقَدْ بَلَغَ هٰذَا الْكَلْبُ مِنَ الْعَطَشِ مِثْلُ الَّذِي كَانَ قَدْ بَلَغَ مِنِّي، فَنَزَلَ الْبِئْرَ فَمَلأَ خُفَّهُ مَاءً ثُمَّ أَمْسَكَهُ بِفِيهِ، حَتَّى رَقِيَ

leather sock with water, and holding it in his mouth, he climbed up and quenched the thirst of the dog. Allâh appreciated his action and forgave his sins." The Companions asked: "Shall we be rewarded for showing kindness to the animals also?" He ﷺ said, "A reward is given in connection with every living creature." [*Al-Bukhârî* and *Muslim*]

فَسَقَى الْكَلْبَ، فَشَكَرَ اللهُ لَهُ فَغَفَرَ لَهُ» قَالُوا: يَا رَسُولَ الله! وَإِنَّ لَنَا فِي الْبَهَائِمِ أَجْرًا؟ فَقَالَ: فِي كُلِّ كَبِدٍ رَطْبَةٍ أَجْرٌ» متفقٌ عَلَيه.

In the narration of *Al-Bukhârî*, the Prophet ﷺ is reported to have said: "Allâh forgave him in appreciation of this act and admitted him to *Jannah*."

وَفِي رِوَايَةٍ لِلْبُخَارِيّ: «فَشَكَرَ اللهُ لَهُ فَغَفَرَ لَه، فَأَدْخَلَهُ الْجَنَّةَ».

Another narration says: "Once a dog was going around a well and was about to die out of thirst, when a prostitute of Banu Isrâel happened to see it. So she took off her leather sock and lowered it into the well. She drew out some water and gave it to the dog to drink. She was forgiven on account of her action."

وَفِي رِوَايَةٍ لَهُمَا: «بَيْنَمَا كَلْبٌ يُطِيفُ بِرَكِيَّةٍ قَدْ كَادَ يَقْتُلُهُ الْعَطَشُ إِذْ رَأَتْهُ بَغِيٌّ مِنْ بَغَايَا بَنِي إِسْرَائِيلَ، فَنَزَعَتْ مُوقَهَا فَاسْتَقَتْ لَهُ بِهِ، فَسَقَتْهُ فَغُفِرَ لَهَا بِهِ».

Commentary:

1. This *Hadîth* emphasizes the importance of kindness to every creature, even animals, because Allâh is pleased with such kindness.

2. Allâh's Quality of mercy and forgiveness is immensely vast. If He wants He may forgive a person even for a minor good deed done by him.

The reward is of the same nature of the Deeds

44. Abû Hurairah رضي الله عنه reported: The Messenger of Allâh ﷺ said, "He who removes from a believer one of his difficulties of this world,

٤٤ - وَعَنْ أَبِي هُرَيْرَةَ رَضِيَ اللهُ عَنْهُ، عَنِ النَّبِيِّ ﷺ قَالَ: «مَنْ نَفَّسَ عَنْ مُؤْمِنٍ كُرْبَةً مِنْ كُرَبِ الدُّنْيَا، نَفَّسَ

Allâh will remove one of his troubles on the Day of Resurrection; and he who gives relief to a hard-pressed person, Allâh will make things easy for him in this life and in the hereafter; he who covers up (the faults and sins) of a Muslim, Allâh will cover up (his faults and sins) in this world and in the Hereafter. Allâh helps His slave as long as the slave helps his brother; and he who treads a path in search of knowledge, Allâh makes easy for him a path leading to *Jannah*. The people who assemble in one of the houses of Allâh, reciting the Book of Allâh, learning it and teaching it, there descends upon them the tranquillity, mercy covers them, the angels flock around them, and Allâh mentions them in the presence of those near Him; and he who lags behind in doing good deeds, his noble lineage will not make him go ahead." [*Muslim*]

اللهُ عَنْهُ كُرْبَةً مِنْ كُرَبِ يَوْمِ الْقِيَامَةِ، وَمَنْ يَسَّرَ عَلَى مُعْسِرٍ يَسَّرَ اللهُ عَلَيْهِ فِي الدُّنْيَا وَالآخِرَةِ، وَمَنْ سَتَرَ مُسْلِمًا سَتَرَهُ اللهُ فِي الدُّنْيَا وَفِي الآخِرَةِ، وَاللهُ فِي عَوْنِ الْعَبْدِ مَا كَانَ الْعَبْدُ فِي عَوْنِ أَخِيهِ، وَمَنْ سَلَكَ طَرِيقًا يَلْتَمِسُ فِيهِ عِلْمًا سَهَّلَ اللهُ لَهُ طَرِيقًا إِلَى الْجَنَّةِ. وَمَا اجْتَمَعَ قَوْمٌ فِي بَيْتٍ مِنْ بُيُوتِ اللهِ تَعَالَى، يَتْلُونَ كِتَابَ اللهِ، وَيَتَدَارَسُونَهُ بَيْنَهُمْ إِلَّا نَزَلَتْ عَلَيْهِمُ السَّكِينَةُ، وَغَشِيَتْهُمُ الرَّحْمَةُ، وَحَفَّتْهُمُ الْمَلائِكَةُ، وَذَكَرَهُمُ اللهُ فِيمَنْ عِنْدَهُ وَمَنْ بَطَّأَ بِهِ عَمَلُهُ لَمْ يُسْرِعْ بِهِ نَسَبُهُ» رَوَاهُ مسلم.

Commentary: Besides other advantages mentioned in this *Hadîth*, we learn the following from it:

1. It is an act of great merit to relieve a Muslim from his financial difficulty.
2. To strive for attaining religious knowledge is a highly meritorious act.
3. To recite the Noble Qur'ân, make arrangement for its study and teaching, and hold meetings for the understanding and elucidation of the message of the Noble Qur'ân are acts of great distinction and reward.

Humbleness is Rewardable

45. Abû Hurairah رضي الله عنه reported: The Messenger of Allâh ﷺ

٤٥ - وَعَنْ أَبِي هُرَيْرَةَ رَضِيَ اللهُ عَنْهُ أَنَّ رَسُولَ اللهِ ﷺ قَالَ: «مَا نَقَصَتْ

صَدَقَةٌ مِنْ مَالٍ، وَمَا زَادَ اللهُ عَبْدًا بِعَفْوٍ إِلَّا عِزًّا، وَمَا تَوَاضَعَ أَحَدٌ للهِ إِلَّا رَفَعَهُ اللهُ» رَوَاهُ مُسْلِم.

said, "Wealth does not diminish by giving *Sadaqah* (charity). Allâh augments the honor of one who forgives; and no one humbles himself for Allâh, but Allâh will exalt him in ranks." [*Muslim*]

Commentary: Apparently giving in *Sadaqah* (charity) decreases wealth, but Allâh fairly compensates an almsgiver by increasing his wealth. Otherwise, he is sure to receive the best recompense in the Hereafter which will make good his loss. Or, Allâh blesses the rest of his wealth in such a way that the sense of loss is removed from his mind. As for a lenient and humble attitude, it is sometimes mistaken by man for his humiliation. But the Messenger of Allâh ﷺ calls such an impression as erroneous. Indeed, humility increases his honor and dignity. And as regards the Hereafter, the best reward is bound to come to him when he will be blessed with spiritual heights.

Helping Others

٤٦ - عَنْ أَبِي هُرَيْرَةَ رَضِيَ اللهُ عَنْهُ قَالَ: قَالَ رَسُولُ اللهِ ﷺ: «كُلُّ سُلَامَى مِنَ النَّاسِ عَلَيْهِ صَدَقَةٌ كُلَّ يَوْمٍ تَطْلُعُ فِيهِ الشَّمْسُ: تَعْدِلُ بَيْنَ الاثْنَيْنِ صَدَقَةٌ، وَتُعِينُ الرَّجُلَ فِي دَابَّتِهِ فَتَحْمِلُهُ عَلَيْهَا، أَوْ تَرْفَعُ لَهُ عَلَيْهَا مَتَاعَهُ صدقةٌ، والكَلِمَةُ الطَّيِّبَةُ صَدَقَةٌ، وَبِكُلِّ خَطْوَةٍ تَمْشِيهَا إِلَى الصَّلَاةِ صَدَقَةٌ، وَتُمِيطُ الأَذَى عَنِ الطَّرِيقِ صَدَقَةٌ» متفقٌ عليه.

رَوَاهُ مُسلم أَيْضًا مِنْ رِوَايَةِ عَائِشَةَ رَضِي الله عَنْهَا قَالَتْ: قَالَ رَسُولُ اللهِ ﷺ: «إِنَّهُ

46. Abû Hurairah رضي الله عنه reported: The Messenger of Allâh ﷺ said, "Every day the sun rises, charity (*Sadaqah*) is due on every joint of a person. Administering justice between two people is a charity; and assisting a man to mount his beast, or helping him load his luggage on it is a charity; and a good word is a charity; and every step that you take (towards the mosque) for *Salât* (prayer) is a charity; and removing harmful things from the road is a charity." [*Al-Bukhârî* and *Muslim*]

In *Muslim* it is reported on the authority of 'Âishah رضي الله عنها that the Messenger of Allāh ﷺ said, "Everyone of the children of Adam has been created with three hundred and sixty joints; so he who declares the Greatness of Allâh (i.e., saying *Allâhu Akbar*), praises Allâh (i.e., *Al-hamdu lillâh*), declares Allâh to be One (i.e., *Lâ ilâha illallâh*), glorifies Allâh (i.e., *Subhān Allāh*), and seeks forgiveness from Allâh (i.e., *Astaghfirullâh*), and removes a stone or thorn or bone from people's path, and enjoins good and forbids evil, to the number of those three hundred and sixty, will come upon the evening that day having rescued himself from Hell."

خُلِقَ كُلُّ إِنْسَانٍ مِنْ بَنِي آدَمَ عَلَى سِتِّينَ وَثَلَاثِمائَةِ مَفْصِلٍ، فَمَنْ كَبَّرَ اللهَ، وَحَمِدَ اللهَ، وَهَلَّلَ اللهَ، وَسَبَّحَ اللهَ واسْتَغْفَرَ اللهَ، وَعَزَلَ حَجَرًا عَنْ طَرِيقِ النَّاسِ أَوْ شَوْكَةً أَوْ عَظْمًا عَنْ طَرِيقِ النَّاسِ، أَوْ أَمَرَ بِمَعْرُوفٍ أَوْ نَهَى عَنْ مُنْكَرٍ، عَدَدَ السِّتِّينَ وَالثَّلَاثمائَةِ، فَإِنَّهُ يُمْسِي يَوْمَئِذٍ وَقَدْ زَحْزَحَ نَفْسَهُ عَنِ النَّارِ».

Commentary: This *Hadîth* informs tells that even a person who does not have the capacity to pay *Sadaqah* (charity, alms, propitiatory offerings, etc.) can also pay it in the manner prescribed above and earn its reward. Moreover, he can also pay alms for the joints in his body.

Honoring Parents' Friends

47. 'Abdullâh bin Dînâr رضي الله عنه reported:' Abdullah bin 'Umar رضي الله عنهما met a bedouin on his way to Makkah, so he greeted him, carried him on the donkey he was riding and gave him the turban he was wearing on his head. Ibn Dînâr said: We said to him: "May Allâh make you pious! Bedouins can be satisfied with anything you give them (i.e., what you have given the bedouin is too much)." Upon this, 'Abdullâh bin 'Umar said: The father of this man was one of

٤٧ - وَعَنْ عبدِ اللهِ بْنِ دِينَارٍ عن عَبْدِاللهِ بْنِ عُمَرَ رَضِيَ اللهُ عَنْهُمَا أَنَّ رَجُلًا مِنَ الأعْرَابِ لَقِيَهُ بِطَرِيقِ مَكَّةَ، فَسَلَّمَ عَلَيْهِ عَبْدُاللهِ بْنُ عُمَرَ، وَحَمَلَهُ عَلَى حِمَارٍ كَانَ يَرْكَبُهُ، وَأَعْطَاهُ عِمَامَةً كَانَتْ عَلَى رَأْسِهِ، قَال ابنُ دِينَارٍ: فَقُلْنَا لَهُ: أَصْلَحَكَ اللهُ إِنَّهُمُ الأَعْرَابُ وَهُمْ يَرْضَوْنَ بِاليَسِيرِ فَقَالَ عَبْدُاللهِ بنُ عُمَرَ: إِنَّ

'Umar's friends whom he loved best, and I heard the Messenger of Allâh saying, "The finest act of goodness is the good treatment of someone whom one's father loves."

Another narration goes: When 'Abdullâh bin 'Umar رضي الله عنهما set out to Makkah, he kept a donkey with him to ride when he would get tired of riding the camel, and had a turban which he tied around his head. One day, as he was riding the donkey, a bedouin happened to pass by him. He ('Abdullâh bin 'Umar) said, "Aren't you so-and-so?" The bedouin said, "Yes." He ('Abdullâh bin 'Umar) gave him his donkey and his turban and said, "Ride this donkey, and tie this turban around your head." Some of his companions said. "May Allâh forgive you. You gave this bedouin the donkey which you enjoyed riding for change, and the turban which you tied around your head." 'Abdullâh bin 'Umar said, "I heard the Messenger of Allâh ﷺ saying, 'The finest act of goodness is the kind treatment of a person to the loved ones of his father after his death,' and the father of this person was a friend of 'Umar رضي الله عنه." [Muslim]

أَبَا هٰذَا كَانَ وُدًّا لِعُمَرَ بْنِ الْخَطَّابِ رَضِيَ الله عَنْهُ وَإِنِّي سَمِعْتُ رَسُولَ الله ﷺ يَقُولُ: «إِنَّ أَبَرَّ الْبِرِّ صِلَةُ الرَّجُلِ أَهْلَ وُدِّ أَبِيهِ».

وَفِي رِوَايَةٍ عَنِ ابْنِ دِينَارٍ عَنِ ابْنِ عُمَرَ أَنَّهُ كَانَ إِذَا خَرَجَ إِلَى مَكَّةَ كَانَ لَهُ حِمَارٌ يَتَرَوَّحُ عَلَيْهِ إِذَا مَلَّ رُكُوبَ الرَّاحِلَةِ، وَعِمَامَةٌ يَشُدُّ بِهَا رَأْسَهُ، فَبَيْنَا هُوَ يَوْمًا عَلَى ذٰلِكَ الْحِمَارِ إِذْ مَرَّ بِهِ أَعْرَابِيٌّ، فَقَالَ: أَلَسْتَ ابْنَ فُلَانِ ابْنِ فُلَانٍ؟ قَالَ: بَلَى. فَأَعْطَاهُ الْحِمَارَ، فَقَالَ: ارْكَبْ هٰذَا، وَأَعْطَاهُ الْعِمَامَةَ وَقَالَ: اشْدُدْ بِهَا رَأْسَكَ، فَقَالَ لَهُ بَعْضُ أَصْحَابِهِ: غَفَرَ اللهُ لَكَ أَعْطَيْتَ هٰذَا الْأَعْرَابِيَّ حِمَارًا كُنْتَ تَرَوَّحُ عَلَيْهِ، وَعِمَامَةً كُنْتَ تَشُدُّ بِهَا رَأْسَكَ؟ فَقَالَ: إِنِّي سَمِعْتُ رَسُولَ الله ﷺ يَقُولُ: «إِنَّ مِنْ أَبَرِّ الْبِرِّ أَنْ يَصِلَ الرَّجُلُ أَهْلَ وُدِّ أَبِيهِ بَعْدَ أَنْ يُوَلِّيَ» وَإِنَّ أَبَاهُ كَانَ صَدِيقًا لِعُمَرَ رَضِيَ الله عَنْهُ، رَوَى هٰذِهِ الرِّوَايَاتِ كُلَّهَا مسلم.

Commentary: This *Hadîth* teaches that after the death of one's parents, one should maintain contact with their friends and treat them nicely. Besides being a great virtue it is warranted by the needs for showing compassion to relatives. To forget friends of one's parents and break contact with them is condemned by the *Sharî'ah*.

Kindness to Parents

48. Abû Usaid Mâlik bin Rabî'ah As-Sâ'idi رضي الله عنه reported: We were sitting with the Messenger of Allâh ﷺ when a man of Banû Salamah came to him and asked, "Oh Messenger of Allâh! Is there any kindness to parents left that I can show to them after their death?" He ﷺ replied, "Yes, to pray for them, supplicate for their forgiveness, fulfil their promises after their death, maintain the ties of kinship which cannot be maintained except through them, and honor their friends." [*Abû Dâwûd*, and graded weak (unauthentic) by Shaikh Al-Albâni.]

٤٨ - وَعَنْ أَبِي أُسَيْدٍ - بِضَمِّ الهَمْزَةِ وَفَتْحِ السِّينِ - مَالِكِ بْنِ رَبِيعَةَ السَّاعِدِيِّ رَضِيَ اللهُ عَنْهُ قَالَ: بَيْنَا نَحْنُ جُلُوسٌ عِنْدَ رَسُولِ اللهِ ﷺ إِذْ جَاءَهُ رَجُلٌ مِنْ بَنِي سَلَمَةَ فَقَالَ: يَا رَسُولَ اللهِ هَلْ بَقِيَ مِنْ بِرِّ أَبَوَيَّ شَيْءٌ أَبَرُّهُمَا بِهِ بَعْدَ مَوْتِهِمَا؟ فَقَالَ: «نَعَمْ، الصَّلاةُ عَلَيْهِمَا، وَالاسْتِغْفَارُ لَهُمَا، وَإِنْفَاذُ عَهْدِهِمَا مِنْ بَعْدِهِمَا، وَصِلَةُ الرَّحِمِ الَّتِي لا تُوصَلُ إِلَّا بِهِمَا، وَإِكْرَامُ صَدِيقِهِمَا» رَوَاهُ أَبُو دَاود.

Commentary: We learn from this *Hadîth* that one should consider the life of one's parents a blessing because their life provides one with an opportunity to serve them wholeheartedly, which is ordained by Allâh. If one wants to be nice to them after their death, one should adopt the methods mentioned in this *Hadîth*. It needs to be noted that it does not mention the ceremonies like recitation of the Noble Qur'ân on the third, seventh and fortieth day after the death of a person, which is practiced in our society. All these methods of conveying the reward of virtuous deeds or rites are wrong for the reason that they are neither helpful for the dead nor the living. What really benefits the dead as well as living, is prayer and begging forgiveness from Allâh. In this *Hadîth*, these have been regarded as acts of beneficence for the deceased parents. It clearly means that the children will be rewarded for the virtuous acts they do for their parents and the status of the deceased parents will also be elevated in the next world. The acceptance of the prayer for the deceased parents is also confirmed from this *Hadîth*, which shows that death brings to an end all the activities, except the following: Firstly, an ongoing *Sadaqah* (*Sadaqah Jâriyah*); like the digging of a well, the building of a mosque, etc.,

Secondly, knowledge which benefits Muslims;

Thirdly, prayers of virtuous offspring.

49. 'Abdullâh bin Mas'ûd رضي الله عنه reported: I asked the Prophet ﷺ, "Which of the deeds is loved most by Allâh?" The Messenger of Allâh ﷺ said, "*Salât at its proper time.*" I asked, "What next?" He ﷺ replied, "*Kindness to parents.*" I asked, "What next?" He replied, "*Jihâd in the way of Allâh.*"

[*Al-Bukhârî* and *Muslim*]

٤٩ - عَنْ عبدِاللهِ بنِ مَسْعُودٍ رَضِيَ الله عَنْهُ قَالَ: سَأَلْتُ النَّبِيَّ ﷺ: أَيُّ الْعَمَلِ أَحَبُّ إِلَى الله تَعَالَى؟ قَالَ: «الصَّلاةُ عَلَى وَقْتِهَا» قُلْتُ: ثُمَّ أَيُّ؟ قَالَ: «بِرُّ الْوَالِدَيْنِ» قُلْتُ: ثُمَّ أَيُّ؟ قَالَ: «الْجِهَادُ فِي سَبِيلِ الله» متفقٌ عَلَيه.

Commentary: Performance of *Salât* at the stated time means its performance in the earliest prescribed time or at least during its stipulated time. One should not give preference to mundane affairs over it. *Salât* and *Jihâd* are the two most meritorious duties of a Muslim. When nice treatment to parents is mentioned along with *Salât* and *Jihâd*, it gives further importance to this injunction.

50. Abû Hurairah رضي الله عنه reported: A person came to the Messenger of Allâh ﷺ and asked, "Who among people is most deserving of my fine treatment?" He ﷺ said, "Your mother." He then said, "Who next?" "Your mother," the Prophet ﷺ replied again. He asked, "Who next?" He (the Prophet ﷺ) said again, "Your mother." He again asked, "Then who?" Thereupon he ﷺ said, "Your father."

In another narration: "O Messenger of Allâh! Who is most deserving of my fine treatment?" He ﷺ said, "Your mother, then your mother, then your

٥٠ - وَعَنْ أَبِي هُرَيْرَةَ رَضِيَ الله عَنْهُ قَالَ: جَاءَ رَجُلٌ إِلَى رَسُولِ الله ﷺ فَقَالَ: يَا رَسُولَ الله مَنْ أَحَقُّ النَّاسِ بِحُسْنِ صَحَابَتِي؟ قَالَ: «أُمُّكَ» قَالَ: ثُمَّ مَنْ؟ قَالَ: «أُمُّكَ» قَالَ: ثُمَّ مَنْ؟ قَالَ: «أُمُّكَ» قَالَ: ثُمَّ مَنْ؟ قَالَ: «أَبُوكَ». متفقٌ عَلَيه.

وَفِي رِوَايَةٍ: يَا رَسُولَ الله مَنْ أَحَقُّ بِحُسْنِ الصُّحْبَةِ؟ قَالَ: «أُمُّكَ، ثُمَّ أُمُّكَ، ثُمَّ أُمُّكَ، ثُمَّ أَبَاكَ، ثُمَّ أَدْنَاكَ أَدْنَاكَ».

Prophet Muḥammad ﷺ especially loved to be among children. One day, he was with a group of children, talking to them and playing with them.

The children were very happy to be with the prophet who was so kind to them.

A man arrived there and watched the children playing and laughing with Muḥammad ﷺ. The man was looking pale and unhappy. Muḥammad ﷺ noticed this, and asked the man why he was unhappy. The man said, "I have ten children and I have never kissed them."

The prophet felt sorry for the man. He told him that loving and caring for children was a blessing from Allāh.

On another occasion, it was very cold so a man made a fire to get warm. But nearby there were many ants. The prophet ﷺ saw the fire and the ants. He was disturbed to see the ants in danger.

He asked the man to put out the fire. The man did as he was asked and when he looked round saw the ants.

The man knew why the prophet ﷺ wanted him to put out the fire.

The prophet said to him, "You will be rewarded by Allāh for your acts of kindness towards His living creatures."

Muḥammad ﷺ asked the stone-hearted Makkans to think again, to give up idol worship and return to the worship of Allāh alone. He had to work very hard to turn the people of Makkah into Muslims. He was able to do it because Allāh's help was with him.

Muḥammad ﷺ

is the last of the prophets and messengers. Allāh completed His guidance for mankind with Muḥammad ﷺ. Islām is this complete guidance.

Muḥammad ﷺ,

the Great Leader and the last messenger of Allāh, lived for 63 years. He died in Madīnah in the year 632 CE. He left us the Qur'ān and his sunnah (life example) for our guidance.

Things to do 7

Answer these questions:

1. When was prophet Muḥammad ﷺ born?
2. Who was Muḥammad's ﷺ father?
3. When did Muḥammad's ﷺ mother die?
4. Who looked after Muḥammad ﷺ after his mother died?
5. Where was Muḥammad ﷺ when the angel Jibrā'īl appeared to him?
6. In which year did Muḥammad ﷺ become the prophet of Allāh?
7. When did the prophet Muḥammad ﷺ die?
8. What did the prophet leave for our guidance?
9. How did Muḥammad ﷺ behave with children?
10. What is the first Arabic sentence that was revealed to Muḥammad ﷺ?

Telling the Truth

Telling the truth is a very good habit. If you always speak the truth, you save yourself from a lot of trouble. Here is the story about a person who did a lot of bad things, but his promise to tell the truth saved him.

Once a man came to the prophet Muḥammad ﷺ and said, "O prophet of Allāh, I have many bad habits. Which of them should I give up first?" The prophet said, "Give up telling lies first and always speak the truth." The man promised to do so and went home.

At night the man was about to go out to steal. Before setting out, he thought for a moment about the promise he made with the prophet." If tomorrow the prophet asks me where I have been, what shall I say? How can I say that I went out stealing? No, I should not say that. But nor can I lie. If I tell the truth, everyone will start hating me and calling me a thief. I would be punished for stealing."

So the man decided not to steal that night, and gave up this bad habit.

The next day he felt like drinking wine, but when he was about to do so he said to himself, "What shall I say to the prophet if he asks me what I did during the day? I cannot tell a lie, and if I speak the truth people will hate me, because a Muslim is not allowed to drink wine." And so he gave up the idea of drinking wine.

In this way, whenever the man thought of doing something bad, he remembered his promise to tell the truth at all times. One by one, he gave up all his bad habits and became a good Muslim and a very good person.

If you always speak the truth, you can be a good person, a good Muslim whom Allāh likes and favours. If Allāh – our Creator – is pleased with us He will reward us with Paradise, which is a place of happiness and joy.

Make a promise: I shall always speak the truth.

Words and Actions Should be the Same

There once was a boy who loved eating sweets. He always asked for sweets from his father. His father was a poor man. He could not always afford sweets for his son. But the little boy did not understand this, and demanded sweets all the time.

The boy's father thought hard about how to stop the child asking for so many sweets. He heard of a great man living nearby at that time who loved and worshipped Allāh very much. The boy's father had an idea. He decided to take the boy to the great man who might be able to persuade the child to stop asking for sweets all the time.

The boy and his father went along to the great man. The father said to him, "O great man, could you ask my son to stop asking for sweets which I cannot afford?" The great man faced a test, because he liked sweets himself. How could he ask the boy to give up asking for sweets? The great man told his father to bring his son back after one month.

During that month, the great man gave up eating sweets, and when the boy and his father returned after a month, the great man said to the boy, "My dear child, will you stop asking for sweets which your father cannot afford to give you?"

From then on, the boy stopped asking for sweets.

The boy's father asked the great man, "Why did you not ask my son to give up asking for sweets when we came to you a month ago?"

The great man replied, "How could I ask a boy to give up sweets when I loved sweets myself? In the last month I gave up eating sweets."

A person's example is much more powerful than just his words. When we ask someone to do something, we must also do it ourselves. We should not ask others to do what we do not do ourselves.

Allāh says in the Qur'ān:
"Why do you say that which you do not do? It is most hateful to Allāh that you say that which you do not do."
(Sūrah 61, verses 2–3)

Always make sure that your words and actions are the same.

Five basic duties of Islām

We are Muslims. We must do some basic duties as Muslims.

What are these basic duties?
These duties are five:

These five duties are called **Arkānul Islām** or Pillars of Islām.

Shahādah
(The declaration of faith)

What is Shahādah?
Shahādah is:

لَآ إِلٰهَ إِلَّا اللّٰهُ مُحَمَّدٌ رَّسُولُ اللّٰهِ

Lā ilāha illallāhu Muḥammadur Rasūlullāh

This means:
There is no god but Allāh;
Muḥammad is the messenger of Allāh.

It Is also called **Al-Kalimatuṭ Ṭaiyibah**

اَلْكَلِمَةُ الطَّيِّبَةُ

Shahādah is the first duty of a Muslim.

A person becomes a Muslim by reciting and believing in the Shahādah. In the Shahādah, we declare that Allāh is our Maker and Lord. He has made us and given us all that we have. We also say in the Shahādah that Muḥammad ﷺ is the messenger of Allāh. He is our model Leader who showed us the right path.

Muḥammad ﷺ was sent to show us the right way and the straight path. He is our Teacher. He is the last and the final of the messengers of Allāh.

We should remember that we must also believe in the angels, the books of Allāh, the day of judgement, destiny·and the life after death.

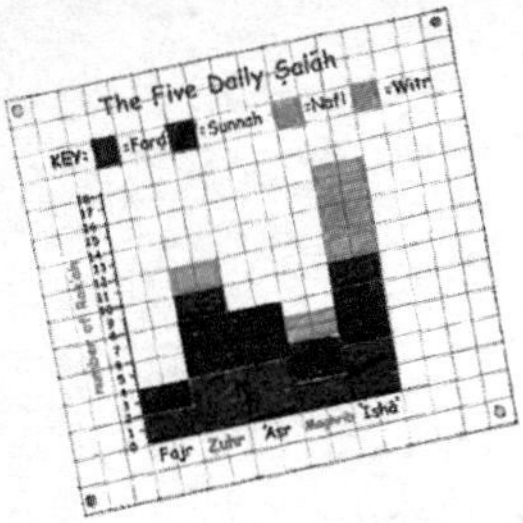

Ṣalāh

(Daily Prayer)

The second important duty of a Muslim is Ṣalāh.

What is Ṣalāh?
Ṣalāh is the five daily prayers which a Muslim must say.

Why should we offer Ṣalāh?
We offer Ṣalāh to remember Allāh, to be close to Him and to gain His favour.

Allāh says in the Qur'ān:
"Establish Ṣalāh to remember Me."
(Sūrah 20, verse 14)

It helps us to get used to doing what Allāh commands us.
It also helps us to do good things and give up bad things.

This is why Allāh says in the Qur'ān:
"Surely Ṣalāh keeps you away from the indecent and the forbidden."
(Sūrah 29, verse 45)

We must pray to be good Muslims. Allāh loves good Muslims.
You cannot be a good Muslim if you do not pray.
Allāh, too, will not be pleased with you.

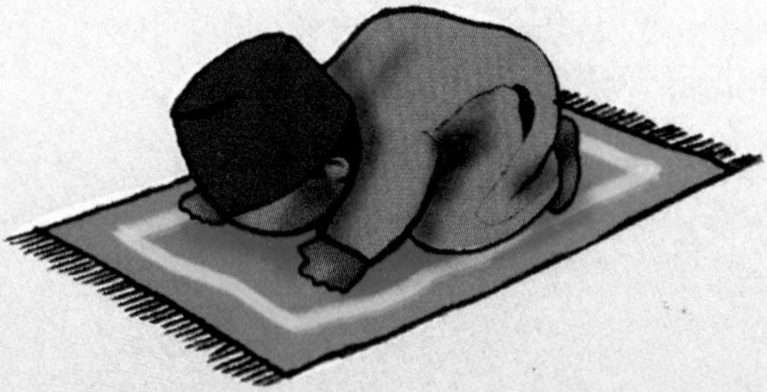

What are the five compulsory prayers that are said each day?
The five prayers are:

1 **Fajr** between dawn and sunrise — صَلَاةُ الْفَجْر

2 **Ẓuhr** between midday and mid-afternoon — صَلَاةُ الظُّهْر

3 **'Aṣr** between mid-afternoon and sunset — صَلَاةُ الْعَصْر

4 **Maghrib** just after sunset — صَلَاةُ الْمَغْرِب

5 **'Ishā'** between nightfall and dawn — صَلَاةُ الْعِشَاء

One unit of prayer is called a **Rak'ah** — رَكْعَة

Compulsory prayer is called **Farḍ** — اَلْفَرْض

Prayers which the prophet said other than Farḍ are called **Sunnah** — اَلسُّنَّة

Optional prayers are called **Nafl** — اَلنَّفْل

The five daily Ṣalāh

Fajr	Ẓuhr	'Aṣr	Maghrib	'Ishā'
2 Sunnah	4 Sunnah	4 Sunnah		4 Sunnah
2 Farḍ	4 Farḍ	4 Farḍ	3 Farḍ	4 Farḍ
	2 Sunnah		2 Sunnah	2 Sunnah
	2 Nafl		2 Nafl	2 Nafl
				3 Witr
				2 Nafl

Ṣalāh test after Ẓuhr- Thursday

We should start praying when we are seven years old.
We must not miss any prayer when we are ten years old.

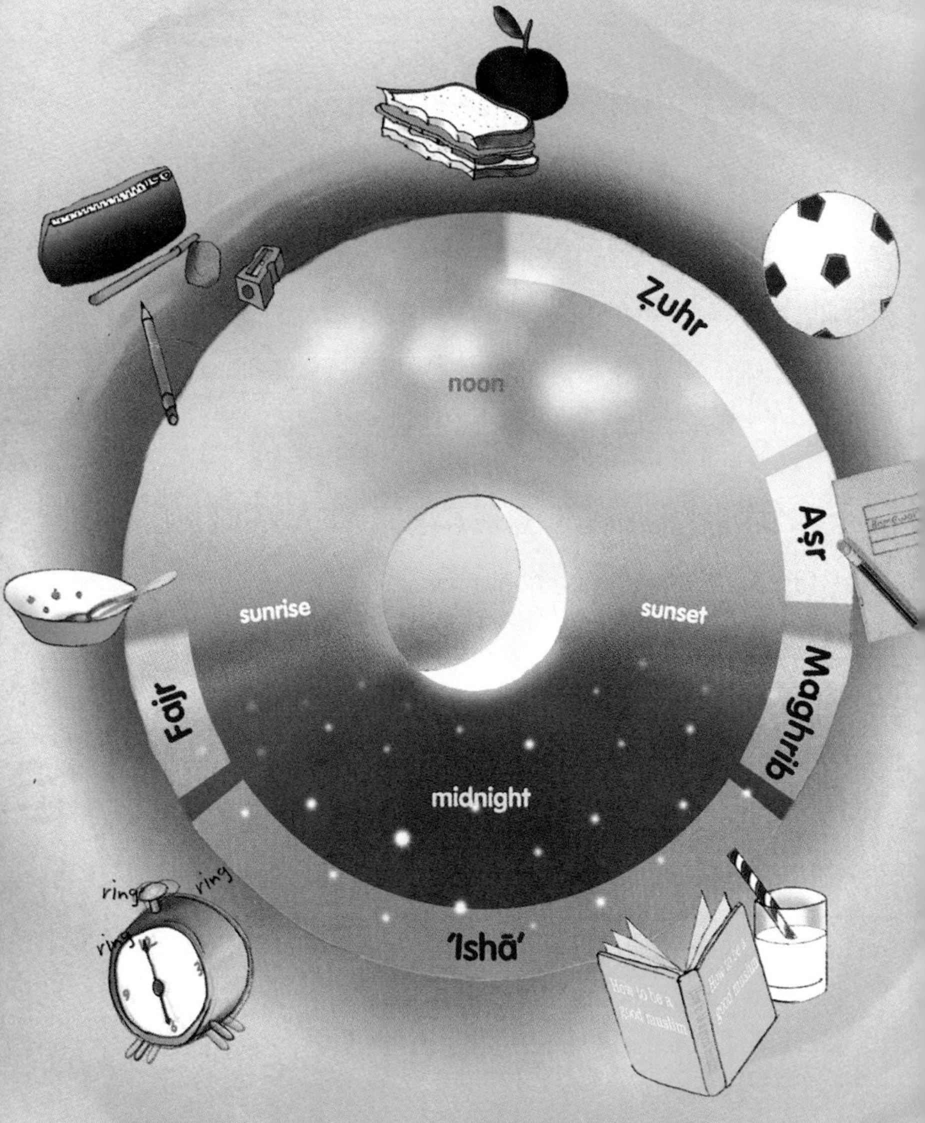

Ṣalāh makes us obedient to Allāh. Allāh will give us a very nice reward for our Ṣalāh in the Ākhirah. He will send us to Jannah.

For details on Ṣalāh, read The Beginner's Book of Ṣalāh by Ghulam Sarwar.

Things to do 8

Answer these questions:

1. What are the five basic duties of a Muslim?
2. What is the declaration of Faith
3. What is Ṣalāh?
4. What are the names of the five daily prayers of Muslims?
5. How many compulsory Rak'ahs of Ṣalāh do Muslims have to pray daily?
6. Why is it important to always tell the truth?
7. Why is it important for us to act upon what we say?

Make your own diagram to show the five basic duties of Islām (see page 48).

Make your own diagram to show the times of the five daily Ṣalāh (see page 52).

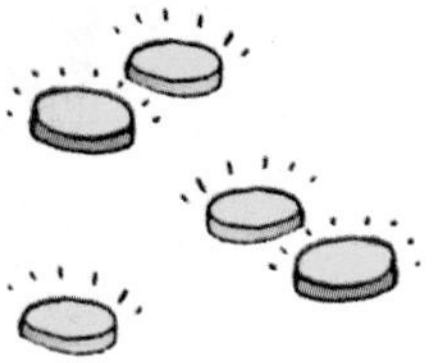

Zakāh
(welfare contribution)

The third basic duty of Islām is Zakāh.

What is Zakāh?
Zakāh is an act of worship ('Ibādah in Arabic), just like Ṣalāh, Ṣawm and Ḥajj. 'Ibādah is any good activity we do to please Allāh. It is the payment of money which a Muslim makes towards the cost of welfare to help people who are needy.

What are the welfare purposes or good causes?
They are: helping the poor, the needy and people in trouble or difficulty.

Who must pay Zakāh?
Zakāh must be paid by those Muslims who have more money than they need to spend. Zakāh is paid on the savings which a Muslim has kept for a whole year without spending.

How much must be paid?
The payment is two and a half percent, which is two and a half pence (cents) for each pound (dollar) on cash and the value of gold and silver jewellery. There is a different rate for cattle a Muslim owns and the crops he has grown.

We and our wealth belong to Allāh. Allāh gave us all that we have. So we must share our extra money with our fellow people who are in hardship.

Zakāh is not the same as charity (Ṣadaqah). Zakāh is a payment we have to make once each year, and is only spent on the special good causes mentioned in the Qur'ān (Sūrah 9, verse 60). Charity is something we choose to give for any good cause at any time. Allāh loves us to give charity too.

Allāh will give us more if we pay Zakāh.

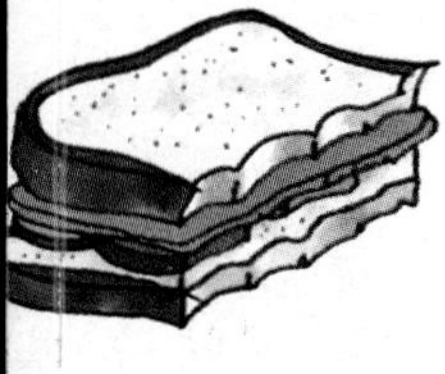

Ṣawm
(fasting)

The fourth basic duty of a Muslim is Ṣawm.

What is Ṣawm?
Ṣawm is fasting in the month of Ramaḍān رَمَضَان every year.

What is fasting?
Fasting is not eating or drinking from dawn to sunset.

Why must we fast?
Allāh told us to fast to gain His favour and keep ourselves away from greed, selfishness and all bad things.

What else is special about the month of Ramaḍān?
In the month of Ramaḍān, after 'Ishā' we pray **Tarāwiḥ** تَرَاوِيح. We take a meal before dawn called **Saḥūr** سَحُور. We break our fast straight after sunset; this is called **Ifṭār** إِفْطَار.

In the month of Ramaḍān there is a very special night. Allāh tells us in the Qur'ān that it is better than a thousand months (Sūrah 97). This night is called **Lailatul Qadr** لَيْلَةُ الْقَدْر (Night of Power). It is one of the last ten nights of the month of Ramaḍān. We should pray as much as we can in this night.

What is the festival that follows Ramaḍān?
The festival after Ramaḍān is called **'Īdul Fiṭr** عِيْدُ الْفِطْر. This is a day of thanksgiving to Allāh. There is a special 'Īd prayer in the morning. It is a happy occasion for Muslims.

We must remember not to lie, break our promises or do bad things while we are fasting in Ramaḍān.

Ramaḍān is a month of great blessings and mercy from Allāh. It is the month of forgiveness.

O Allāh, help us to fast in Ramaḍān to please you.

Ḥajj

(pilgrimage to Makkah)

Ḥajj is the fifth basic duty of Islām.

What is Ḥajj?

Ḥajj is a visit to the Ka'bah اَلْكَعْبَة in Makkah during the month of Dhul Ḥijjah, by those Muslims who can afford the trip. A Muslim tries to make pilgrimage at least once in a lifetime. Ḥajj is an act of worship عِبَادَة ('Ibādah in Arabic). 'Ibādah is any good activity we do to please Allāh.

What is the Ka'bah?

The Ka'bah is the House of Allāh (Baitullāh in Arabic) in Makkah. It is a cube-shaped building covered by a large black cloth. Muslims must face towards the Ka'bah at the time of Ṣalāh. This direction we face is called the Qiblah.

Who built the Ka'bah?

It was built by the first prophet, Ādam (عليه السلام). It was rebuilt by the Prophets Ibrāhīm (عليه السلام) and Ismā'īl (عليه السلام). It is the first house built on earth for the worship of Allāh. Ḥajj is a great event for the Muslims. During Ḥajj, Muslims from all over the world get together in Makkah. It's a yearly gathering of Muslims.

There is a festival which comes during Ḥajj. This festival is called **'Īdul Aḍḥā** عِيدُ الأَضْحَى. There is a special 'Īd prayer in the morning. On this day we remember when prophet Ibrāhīm (عليه السلام) was ready to obey Allāh and sacrifice his son prophet Ismā'īl (عليه السلام).

Ḥajj teaches us that we belong to Allāh only. So, we must always do as Allāh commands.

Things to do 9

Answer these questions:

1. What is Zakāh?
2. Why do you think it is important to give Zakāh?
3. How much Zakāh must we pay on our savings?
4. Who has given us our wealth?
5. What is Ṣawm?
6. Why do we fast?
7. What is Lailatul Qadr?
8. What are the two festivals of Islām?
9. What is Ḥajj?
10. Where do we go for Ḥajj?
11. Where is the Ka'bah?
12. Which direction do we face when saying our Ṣalāh?

Write a short story about either 'Īdul Fiṭr or 'Īdul Aḍḥā.

Four Sūrahs of the Qur'ān

1 Al-Fātiḥah

بِسْمِ ٱللَّهِ ٱلرَّحْمَٰنِ ٱلرَّحِيمِ ١

ٱلْحَمْدُ لِلَّهِ رَبِّ ٱلْعَٰلَمِينَ ٢

ٱلرَّحْمَٰنِ ٱلرَّحِيمِ ٣

مَٰلِكِ يَوْمِ ٱلدِّينِ ٤

إِيَّاكَ نَعْبُدُ وَإِيَّاكَ نَسْتَعِينُ ٥

ٱهْدِنَا ٱلصِّرَٰطَ ٱلْمُسْتَقِيمَ ٦

صِرَٰطَ ٱلَّذِينَ أَنْعَمْتَ عَلَيْهِمْ

غَيْرِ ٱلْمَغْضُوبِ عَلَيْهِمْ وَلَا ٱلضَّآلِّينَ ٧

Bismillāhir rahmānir rahīm.	In the name of Allāh, the Most Merciful, the Most Kind.
Alḥamdu lillāhi rabbil 'ālamīn.	All praise is for Allāh, the Lord of the Universe.
Ar-raḥmānir raḥīm.	The Most Merciful, the Most Kind.
Māliki yawmid dīn.	Master of the Day of Judgement.
Iyyāka na'budu wa iyyāka nasta'īn.	You alone we worship, from You alone we seek help.
Ihdinaṣ ṣirāṭal mustaqīm.	Guide us along the straight path.
Ṣirāṭal ladhīna an'amta 'alaihim,	The path of those whom You have favoured,
ghairil maghḍūbi 'alaihim wa laḍ ḍāllīn.	not of those who earned Your anger nor of those who went astray (or who are misguided).

2 Al-Ikhlāṣ

بِسْمِ ٱللَّهِ ٱلرَّحْمَٰنِ ٱلرَّحِيمِ

قُلْ هُوَ ٱللَّهُ أَحَدٌ ﴿١﴾

ٱللَّهُ ٱلصَّمَدُ ﴿٢﴾

لَمْ يَلِدْ وَلَمْ يُولَدْ ﴿٣﴾

وَلَمْ يَكُن لَّهُۥ كُفُوًا أَحَدٌۢ ﴿٤﴾

Bismillāhir rahmānir rahīm.	In the name of Allāh, the Most Merciful, the Most Kind.
Qul huwallāhu ahad.	Say, He is Allāh, the One.
Allāhuṣ ṣamad.	Allāh is Eternal and Absolute.
Lam yalid wa lam yūlad.	None is born of Him nor is He born.
Wa lam yakul lahū kufuwan ahad.	And there is none like Him.

3 Al-Kawthar

بِسْمِ ٱللَّهِ ٱلرَّحْمَٰنِ ٱلرَّحِيمِ

إِنَّآ أَعْطَيْنَٰكَ ٱلْكَوْثَرَ ﴿١﴾

فَصَلِّ لِرَبِّكَ وَٱنْحَرْ ﴿٢﴾

إِنَّ شَانِئَكَ هُوَ ٱلْأَبْتَرُ ﴿٣﴾

Bismillāhir rahmānir rahīm.	In the name of Allāh, the Most Merciful, the Most Kind.
Innā a'ṭaināka l kawthar.	Indeed we have given you the Kawthar (Fountain or Abundance).
Faṣalli lirabbika wanḥar.	So pray to your Lord and make sacrifice.
Inna shāni'aka huwal abtar.	Surely your hater is the one cut off (i.e. without an heir).

4 Al-'Aṣr

بِسْمِ اللّٰهِ الرَّحْمٰنِ الرَّحِيمِ

وَالْعَصْرِ ۝

إِنَّ الْإِنسَـٰنَ لَفِى خُسْرٍ ۝

إِلَّا الَّذِينَ ءَامَنُواْ وَعَمِلُواْ الصَّـٰلِحَـٰتِ

وَتَوَاصَوْاْ بِالْحَقِّ وَتَوَاصَوْاْ بِالصَّبْرِ ۝

Bismillāhir raḥmānir raḥīm	In the name of Allāh, the Most Merciful, the Most Kind.
Wal 'aṣr! Innal insāna lafī khusr,	I swear by the flight of time! Surely mankind is in loss,
illal ladhīna āmanū wa 'amiluṣ ṣāliḥāti	except those who have faith and do good works,
wa tawāṣaw bil ḥaqqi	and encourage one another to follow the Truth
wa tawāṣaw biṣ ṣabr.	and encourage one another to be patient.

Islamic Manners

A Muslim says:

Bismillāh بِسْمِ اللهِ
(in the name of Allāh) when doing something.

Assalāmu 'Alaikum اَلسَّلَامُ عَلَيْكُمْ
(peace be on you) when meeting a Muslim.

Wa'alaikumus salām وَعَلَيْكُمُ السَّلَامُ
(peace be on you too) in reply.

In shā' Allāh إِنْ شَاءَ اللهُ
(if Allāh wishes) when hoping to do something.

Subḥānallāh سُبْحَانَ اللهِ
(Glory to Allāh) to praise someone.

Mā shā Allāh مَا شَاءَ اللهُ
(what Allāh likes) in appreciation.

Fī Āmānillāh فِيْ أَمَانِ اللهِ
(in the protection of Allāh) when seeing someone off.

Jazākallāhu Khairan جَزَاكَ اللهُ خَيْرًا
(may Allāh give you the best reward) to thank someone.

Tawakkaltu 'Alallāh تَوَكَّلْتُ عَلَى اللهِ
(I rely on Allāh) to solve a problem.

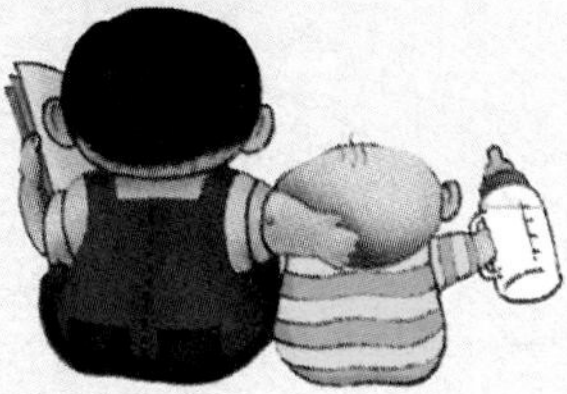

Lā ilāha illallāh لَآ إِلَهَ إِلَّا ٱللّٰهُ
(there is no god but Allāh) when getting up in the morning.

Alḥamdu lillāh اَلْحَمْدُ لِلّٰهِ
(praise be to Allāh) when sneezing.

Yarḥamukallāh يَرْحَمُكَ ٱللّٰهُ
(may Allāh bless you) when hearing someone sneeze.

Āmīn آمِين
(accept our prayer) when joining a Du'ā'.

Yā Allāh يَا أَللّٰهُ
(O Allāh) when in pain or distress.

Astaghfirullāh أَسْتَغْفِرُ ٱللّٰهَ
(I ask Allāh to forgive me) to be sorry for a bad action.

Na'ūdhubillāh نَعُوذُ بِٱللّٰهِ
(we seek refuge with Allāh) to show dislike.

Innā lillāhi wa innā ilaihi rāji'ūn إِنَّا لِلّٰهِ وَإِنَّآ إِلَيْهِ رَاجِعُونَ
(We are for Allāh and to Him we will return)
on the news of the death of a Muslim.

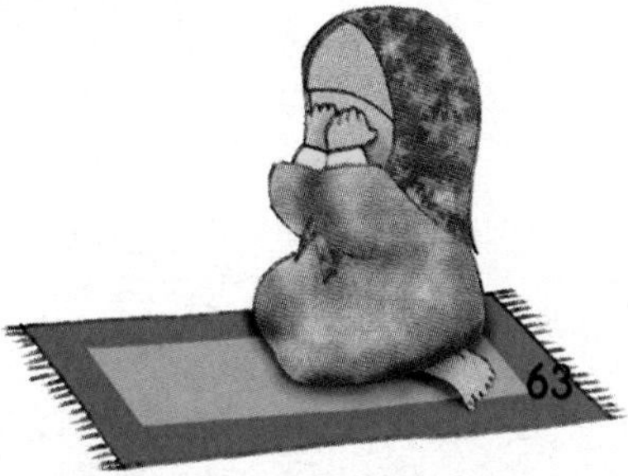

Islāmic Months

Muḥarram	1	مُحَرَّم
Ṣafar	2	صَفَر
Rabī'ul Awwal	3	رَبِيعُ الْأَوَّل
Rabī'ul Ākhir	4	رَبِيعُ الْآخِر
Jumādal Ūlā	5	جُمَادَى الْأُولَى
Jumādal Ākhirah	6	جُمَادَى الْآخِرَة
Rajab	7	رَجَب
Sha'bān	8	شَعْبَان
Ramaḍān	9	رَمَضَان
Shawwāl	10	شَوَّال
Dhul Qa'dah	11	ذُو الْقَعْدَة
Dhul Ḥijjah	12	ذُو الْحِجَّة

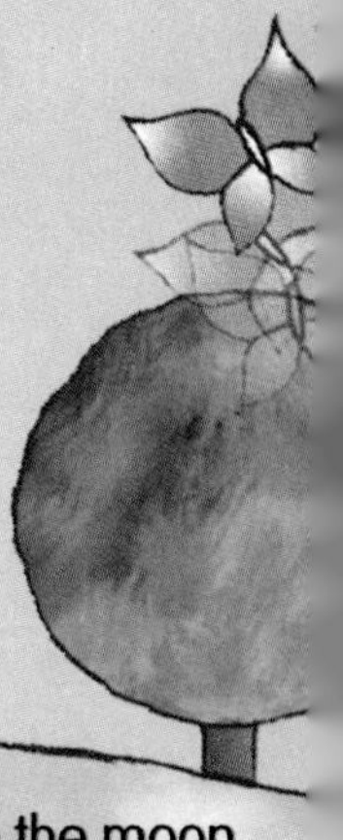

The twelve Islāmic months are counted according to the moon. They are lunar months.

An Islāmic year is a lunar year and has 354 or 355 days. The Christian or Gregorian year depends on the sun. It is a solar year. A solar year has 365 or 366 days.

All Islāmic festivals are observed according to the actual sighting of the moon. That is why Islāmic festival dates are not the same.